Pastoral Supervision

Creativity in Action

Pastoral Supervision
Creativity in Action

with poetry and creative writing by

Liz Crumlish

friends and graduates of the

Institute of Pastoral Supervision & Reflective Practice

IPSRP Publications

First published 2021

Copyright © Michael Paterson & Liz Crumlish 2021

The moral right of the authors has been asserted

For permission to quote from this book please email

enquiries@ipsrp.org.uk

For all
who have risked being creative with us,
made their mark and drawn with us,
created sound and sang with us,
moved and danced with us,
told stories and wrote new endings with us
and brought life and practice
into glorious technicolour.

'We are each other's wind resistance
and we will not make it on our own'

~ Karine Polwarth
Wind Resistance

Tell all the truth but tell it slant —
Success in Circuit lies
Too bright for our infirm Delight
The Truth's superb surprise

~ Emily Dickinson

Creative action methods free us from the tunnel of words to find colour, energy, creativity and a sense of mystery which is so often lacking in the practice of supervision. Visual and active supervision carries new meaning out of the dark and says "Boo!"'

~ Antony Williams

God needs jugglers and high wire artistes - sequinned, sparkling and dancing on the void - if theology is to measure up at all to the magnificent God whose gambling habits and sleights of hand boggle our simple minds.

~ Sara Maitland

Acknowledgments

This book is not only *about* creativity but is also the fruit *of* creativity. Over the last twenty one years I have been training supervisors in the UK, in Malta and in Australia. Whether meeting in person or online, creative action methods have featured prominently in every event. At one stage I ran a Diploma in Creative Supervision but brought that course to an end when the penny dropped that every course I ran, no matter what I called it, was not only shot through with creativity but also resulted in creative outpourings from participants.

In the early days, assignments were fairly traditional: case studies; theoretical essays etc but even then, students would slip in a poem, a piece of music or a photograph of a visual installation they had created in response to some aspect of supervisory theory or practice. In more recent years, thanks to Bobby Moore's wisdom[1], I abandoned traditional forms of assessment in favour of Reflexive Learning Notes which could be creatively or traditionally presented. It is a source of enormous delight that almost every poem you will read in this book is a distilled form of transformative learning originally submitted for assessment by one of our students.

Over the years, IPSRP courses have been enriched by the lively engagement of students drawn from a wide range of caring professions, each with their own body of literature, lenses of interpretation, hobby horses and

---

[1] Moore, B. (2016) *Reflexive Supervision: A workbook for Learning within and across Professions*, KDP.

blind spots. To date our alumni include adult educators, art therapists, chaplains, children's support workers, clergy, coaches, community activists, counsellors, critical incident stress management facilitators, dance movement psychotherapists, dramatherapists, faith leaders, music therapists, nurses, play therapists, psychodramatists, religious sisters, social workers, therapeutic support workers and university lecturers. Across the spiritual traditions our graduates include Buddhists, Christians, Humanists, Jews, One Spirit celebrants and Sufis working in health care chaplaincy, prison chaplaincy, spiritual accompaniment, retreat work, community leadership and formation.

Not only have course graduates contributed their creative writing in this volume, they have also offered invaluable guidance in its contents. A huge thank you to those who kept me right: to Aisling Vorster and Kristin MacDonald (sound & music); Fiona Kernohan and Lynne Grahame (art & imagery); Julie Joseph (embodiment & movement); Suzie Aitken & Stephanie Turner (drama & role).

I am equally indebted to Markus Lange, whose life and work as a rabbi and dramatherapist embodies what this book is about and whose close reading of the text saved you finding my mistakes.

Finally, a huge thank you to Jessica Osborne whose wisdom, collegiality, and friendship have shaped me over the last thirty years. I couldn't ask for a more loving critical-friendship or editorial eye.

Michael Paterson, June 2021

Contents

Introduction
Creativity: A true story	9
What is supervision?	14
What makes it pastoral?	16
Soul, role and context	18

Part One
The Supervisory Relationship
The first meeting	36
A covenant for supervision	39
In the space between us	40
When to introduce creativity	42
When the unconscious presents	46
The Seven Eyes	47
How much of me should show up?	49
Reviewing the relationship	51
Power and vulnerability	53
When things go wrong	57
Endings	60

Part Two
The Supervisory Process
Three levels of seeing	63
Listening to interrupt	69
Listening to understand	70
Listening to ignite	71
A Sat Nav for supervision	75
Hosting & Containing	77
Eliciting & Focusing	81
Exploring & Imagining	83
Tracking & Monitoring	85
Bridging & Enacting	87
Reviewing & Closing	90

Part Three
Creative Modalities in Supervision
Projective modalities	96
Embodied modalities	98
Role modalities	98
Factors to consider	99
Objection: I am just not creative	102
Objection: I don't have time	103
Objection: Creative modalities will do supervisors out of a job	104
Matching modality to supervisory issues	104
Hints in language	106
Hints in content	108
Let the creativity do the talking	112
Assembling a creative kit	114

Part Four
Creative Supervision in Practice

Imagery & Art 120
Using imagery to find focus	121
Creating visual images	122
Focal points for exploring drawings	125
Guided drawing	126
Photography	128
Working with textiles	129
Supervision and weaving	130
Soul Collage®	131

Sound & Music 136
- Sound in preparation 137
- Hosting 139
- Eliciting and focusing 140
- Sound in exploring 142
- Music making in exploring 141
- Using sound for soul, role and context 143
- Assembling a sound collection 145

Embodiment & Movement 147
- Embodied ways of preparing 148
- Embodied beginnings 151
- Embodied supervision outdoors 152
- Embodiment in eliciting and focusing 153
- Embodied signals 154
- Embodied forms of exploring 155
- Somatic Resonance 156
- Exploring the Felt Sense 158

Drama & Role 162
- Role reversal 164
- Working with parts of the self 167
- Chair work 168
- Supervision and experimentation 169
- Inner Wise Guide 171
- Body Sculpting 174
- Dramatized bridging and enacting 174

Language & Story 178
- Clean language 179
- Language in eliciting and focusing 181
- Six minute journaling 183
- Ink polaroids 184
- Writing a way into supervision 184
- Language in exploring and imagining 187

Write in pencil	188
Writing a different ending	189
Working with stories in supervision	193
Fairy tales in supervision	198

Multimodal exploration   202
Individual supervision	203
Four Elements for group supervision	205

Online Supervision   211
Factors to consider	211
Pre-session preparation	212
Technology	213
Environment	213
Impact on the relationship	214

Reading Further

Reading about Pastoral Supervision	221
Reading about Creativity in Supervision	222
Reading about Supervision in general	223

Indices

Author Index	225
Subject Index	228
Poems by first line	232

List of Contributors	234
About the authors	240
About the Institute of Pastoral Supervision	241

*'To be fully seen is a rare
and transformative gift.'*

Mirabai Starr - Wild Mercy

When I can "get over myself"
enough to make room for you
When I can hollow out
a you- shaped space
into which you feel the warmth of invitation
When I can sit side by side with you
in the awareness
that nothing is lost
but that all is gained
in mutual encounter
That
Right there
Is a transformative gift.
And it may even be
that the work made possible
in that rare gift of
you-shaped space
is secondary
to the gift of contemplative seeing
that looks in love
and looks again
To be fully seen
An aspirational
and inspirational
gift without measure.

~ Liz Crumlish

The way ahead lies trapped

The way ahead lies trapped within
waiting to be released
by a skilful conversation
that gets to the heart of the matter
unwrapping, layer by layer
wisdom that is rooted in experience.
Lying dormant, it needs only a trickle of light
to begin the process of awakening
and, once begun, like an energy saving bulb,
it gathers momentum
until all is revealed
- or at least enough to move forward
And each of the parties involved in encounter
proceeds with slightly less caution
buoyed up by the discovery
that it is OK to experiment
it is OK to risk
because each is not only held
but encouraged and enabled to fly.

~ Liz Crumlish

Introduction

For the last twelve months I have been living with Long Covid. Talking leaves me breathless. My head, my muscles and my bones ache. My mental health has been battered. And yet my soul is more alive than ever. Life pared down to the bare minimum demands a discerning answer to a demanding question: 'What will you use your breath for?'

I take the question everywhere: to prayer, to journaling, to walks by the sea. The question has become the soundtrack of my life. No surprise then that I also take it to supervision.

'I want to explore what I will use my breath for now that I have less of it than ever.'

As a priest, divorced by lockdown from people and pulpit, my head tells me that I *should* return to ministry.

As a supervisor supporting those who have borne the brunt at the front-line, my superego tells me I *should* go on supporting.

As a husband, grateful for the care which has nurtured me back from the brink, love tells me that it is now *my* turn to do the caring.

So many voices. So many responses. My head hurts.

I take my hurting head to supervision with Liz.

'I want to explore what I will use my breath for now that I have less of it than ever' I begin.

'How would you like to explore it' Liz asks.

'I don't know …. my head is going round in circles.'

'How about we change gear' she asks 'and take a break from thinking?'

I willingly consent.

'How about you look around your room (we were meeting on Zoom) and see where your eye lands?'

My room is full of 'stuff': chairs, cushions, curtains, desk, books, photographs … I also have a box of stuff that I use in supervision: figurines, image cards, ribbons, cloths, stones, buttons, plastic animals, rubber bands, a compass … I begin to rummage.

My eye lands on some plastic palm trees and a collection of small stones collected from the beach.

Carefully, I position the trees, north, south, east and west. I have no idea why I have chosen them, far less why I am arranging them in this way but know that the objects are doing the talking.

10

I place some stones randomly at the base of each tree.

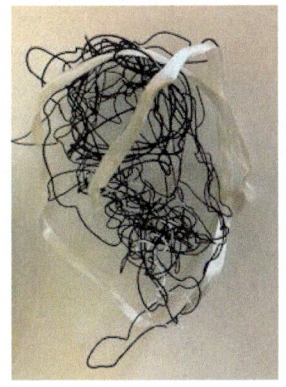

I rummage again through my drawer and this time pull out a scrunched-up piece of wire retrieved from a spiral bound note- book. Today it serves as barbed wire.

I then pick out a ribbon.

'Barbed wire and ribbon? That's curious' I say. Liz says nothing.

Again, without knowing why, I wrap the barbed wire around the tree facing west. It topples over. I drag it out of sight. Next, I wrap the ribbon around the tree facing east. It too topples over. It too gets discarded.

'What do you see now as you look at your question?' Liz asks.

'I notice the space opens up when there is less to take in' I reply.

'And how does that relate to how you will use your breath?' she asks.

'It makes me smile'.

My eyes are fixed on the space that has opened up before my eyes.

I feel the smile spread across my face.

My shoulders lower.

My jaw relaxes.

I rummage once more and pull out a plastic flower.

'I didn't know I had that' I announce, 'I mean I have had this stuff for years, but I can honestly say I have never seen that flower before.'

I position the flower at the base of the palm tree and gaze at the juxtaposition: a tall iridescent palm tree with a delicate purple flower at its base.

'They shouldn't belong together' I say, 'they come from different worlds and different climates yet here they are and I like what I see.'

'What do you see?' Liz asks.

'Colour and vibrancy … strange juxtapositions …

I thought that having less breath meant I was going to have to let go of things, but right now, I have found something I didn't even know I had – a purple flower – and I can't take my eyes off it.

What if it's about retrieving what I already have and have overlooked?'

I logged onto the session with a story of loss.

I'm logging off with the realization of something found.'

'How will you hang on to what you have found here today?' Liz asks.

'I'm going to get some blutac and stick the tree and the flower on my desk for a while. I feel the need to let them speak to me over the next week or so to see where this discovery takes me.'

'Sounds like we are done then' says Liz.

'We certainly are' I reply.

What do I mean by supervision?

The story you have just read underlines the truth of John Patton's comment that 'We don't take cases to supervision. We are the case!'[2] As a counsellor, my first experience of supervision was of casework management. For three weeks of the month, I would do my best in one to one client work and then in the fourth week show up at my supervisor's house, give an account of how I was getting on with each of my clients, seek guidance on how to serve them better and leave ready to apply my newly acquired wisdom.

Later, as I began to trust my own instincts as a supervisor, I noticed that I was less focused on the work that supervisees brought and much more interested in the workers themselves. What impact was the work having on them? What enabled and disabled them to provide the care they offered etc. After years of experimentation, I have now come to an understanding of supervision which I would encapsulate as follows:

> Supervision is a facilitated, intentional and sustained conversation between a person's
> **Soul, Role and Context**
> in which attention is paid
> to the worker, the work
> and those impacted by the work.

---

[2] John Patton (2012) 'Embodying Wisdom: Pastoral Proverbs for Reflective Practice', *Reflective Practice: Formation and Supervision in Ministry*, Vol. 32, 136.

The conversational nature of supervision challenges the inherent power dynamics between helper and helped and allows each party to bring wisdom to the table. Traditional understandings of supervision typically ground the authority for supervision within the supervisor's knowledge, skill, or experience. What I am proposing is that the effective supervisor is someone who can facilitate the kinds of conversations which enable the supervisee to access their own knowledge, skills and experience (things they had all the time but were, temporarily, unable to access). That wisdom arises from a courageous conversation between a person's soul (their vocational or motivational drivers), their role (the post they hold with its concomitant expectations and responsibilities) and their context (the people, the dynamics and the nitty gritty circumstances in which their work takes place).

What supervisees have taught me over and over again is that joy and fulfilment at work arise from there being sufficient harmony between all three – soul, role and context. So, for example, someone with a deep sense of social justice (soul) who gets appointed to a community development post (role) in a deprived community setting where staff collaborate well together and welcome new ways of thinking and doing (context) is likely to find their work meaningful and satisfying.

Having soul, role and context in sufficient harmony does not mean chasing the ideal job in the ideal setting with the ideal people. The emphasis is on 'sufficient'. Sadly, what supervisees have also taught me is that dissatisfaction and ultimately burnout at work arises when practitioners are unable to bring their personal motivation (soul), the actual job they find themselves in (role) and the nitty gritty realities (the vagaries of context) into sufficient dialogue and equilibrium. So, for example, a deeply compassionate nurse who finds herself in a clinical setting in which relationships are toxic and paperwork is given a higher value than 'people work' is likely to struggle to bring her soul, role and context into harmonic dialogue with each other.

The wise supervisor knows the pitfalls of such an approach. To only focus on soul in such situations would be to default to offering spiritual direction or life coaching. To only focus on role, would be to usurp the role of the line manager or HR department. And to only focus on context would be to abdicate the role of supervisor for that of systems analyst. The interweaving of all three takes knowledge, skill, and experience. It demands clarity of role and purpose, and it takes bucket loads of courage.

What makes supervision pastoral?

Two views can be found in the literature as to what makes supervision 'pastoral'. The dominant view understands 'pastoral' as pertaining to the life and practices of the Abrahamic faith communities. Pastoral describes the ways in which the community of faith leads, guides, and sustains its people in good times and in bad. It has a concern for nurturing the young, caring for the sick, supporting the troubled, fostering good relationships and ultimately being there at life's end for the dying and thereafter for the bereaved. Not surprisingly, much of the literature of this kind of pastoral supervision has been written by people of faith who want to support religious leaders in the work they do.[3]

The second emerging understanding of what makes supervision 'pastoral' arises from a feminist, liberationist reading of sacred texts which challenges the individual/deficit nexus of pastoral care *(helping needy people one at a time)* and homes in on how individuals flounder and flourish in community. Within this framework of understanding, supervision is pastoral when it is thoroughly committed to well-being at personal, client and systemic levels:

- the personal wellbeing of the supervisee;
- the wellbeing of those for whom the supervisee cares;
- and the systemic wellbeing of the organisation within which the supervisee works.

That wider understanding of 'pastoral' extends the supervisor's role beyond the softer edges of care and support, nurture, and guidance to the political edges of speaking truth to power and challenging whatever impedes human fulfilment and community cohesion.[4]

---

[3] Examples include Pohly, Leach and Paterson, Paterson and Rose, Leach. Full details in Bibliography. Geoff Broughton offers an interesting alternative: supervision is pastoral when it attends to faith, hope and love see What is "pastoral" about supervision? A Christological proposal, *St Mark's Review* No. 254, December 2020 (4) 9-22.

[4] For a more extensive discussion of this viewpoint see Michael Paterson (2020) *Between a Rock and a Hard Place: Pastoral Supervision Revisited and Revisioned*, Edinburgh: IPSRP

Show me your soul

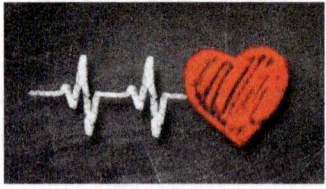

If supervision is about caseload management, then I need someone who has the skills to help me unpack and offload my cases. But if supervision is about soul, role and context, a whole new skill set will be required. The skill to know, from up close, deeply personal familiarity that:

> The soul is like a wild animal—tough, resilient, savvy, self-sufficient and yet exceedingly shy. If we want to see a wild animal, the last thing we should do is to go crashing through the woods, shouting for the creature to come out. But if we are willing to walk quietly into the woods and sit silently for an hour or two at the base of a tree, the creature we are waiting for may well emerge, and out of the corner of an eye we will catch a glimpse of the precious wildness we seek.'[5]

In matters of the soul, second-hand knowledge acquired from books or training will not do. Supervisees need to know that their supervisors know the wildness of the soul and its tendency to only emerge when it is safe to do so. Some do that through words. Others do it by 'sitting silently for an hour or so ... waiting for the creature to emerge.' Finding language for the shy wildness of the soul comes naturally to poets. For many

---

[5] Parker J. Palmer (2004) *A Hidden Wholeness: The Journey Toward an Undivided Life*, San Francisco: JosseyBass.

lesser mortals it is elusive and yet imagery, music, nature befriend our unknowing. How many modern day parables begin 'it's like…?'

Asking supervisees to show their soul can be daunting. Some will quickly resort to a biblical text which has been personally adopted as a mission statement for their life: 'I have come that you would have life and have it abundantly[6] just about sums it up' one person might say while another might choose a line of poetry as their personal mantra: 'I took the road less travelled and that made all the difference.'[7] Some supervisees will simply not be able to find an answer commensurate with the question. 'I wonder if you would like to flick through these image cards and pick out any which resonate with your soul today?' or 'Have you ever read a book and found yourself identifying with one of the characters? Tell me about that character. And tell me what it is about that character that you identify with'.

Even when someone does have words to express their soul, the rational mind may get in the way of them really accessing their truest feelings on any given day. In the supervision example with which I opened this chapter, my head, heart and superego were all telling me what I ought to do and simply adding to the brain fog rather than helping my savvy yet exceedingly shy soul to come out. As someone who can drown in words, I needed another route by which to access the wisdom which I was unable to access on my own.

---

[6] John 10.10
[7] Robert Frost (1915) 'The road not taken'

A second issue highlighted by the supervision scenario with which this chapter opens, is that supervision is not dependent on shared understanding. Many supervisors have uncritically adopted the myth that the more we understand the more able we will be to help. This is simply not true. The supervision session I recounted lasted about eight minutes in total. Had Liz (my supervisor) needed to understand me, rather than facilitate my self-discovery through the largely non-verbal process she offered, I am sure I could have filled the hour with details about my health, the roles I had pre-Covid, the ones I thought I might give up easily, those I would be more reluctant to relinquish etc. but I wonder what I would have gained. Had I done that, I am sure I would have felt flat having used all my time and energy to bring my supervisor up to speed with things I knew already. That would have been supervision as information exchange. What Liz offered me was supervision as the pursuit of transformative insight. Given the importance of the soul finding expression in the role, finding a supervisory modality that enables wisdom to emerge rather than for information to be exchanged is crucially important.

Hopefully you noticed just how little the supervisor actually said in that scenario. Soul, role and context supervision is more about facilitating a conversation between a supervisee and their soul's expression in role and context than it is about fostering a conversation between the supervisee and the supervisor. In this kind of work, supervisors are facilitators not interpreters.

Show me your role

'I wonder if you could find a way to show me your role?' asks the supervisor.

'You can use anything that's here. Words, crayons, objects, cloths … Or you might prefer to think of a line from a song or a TV advert. Give your imagination free range.'

Like many supervisees, my roles are multiple and not singular. In church I am the assistant priest which means I have responsibility but not authority. As a trainer I am peer to two colleagues, an authority figure some students, a supporter and coach to others. As a husband, I am a partner, a collaborator, a listening ear, but also someone who needs cared for.

'Show me your role' asks the supervisor. 'Which one?' I reply.

'Whichever one is most relevant to the issue you are bringing to supervision today.'

My focus narrows. Had I come to supervision yesterday I would have been looking at issue X but life has moved on since then and now I want to look at issue Y.

'I'm thinking about my role as a trainer today' I begin 'and the thing that has just popped into my head is a TV advert with the slogan 'Should've gone to Specsavers'.

And with that we are in. The session has begun.

21

Show me your context

The impact of context on practice has really come to the fore in the last decade. In recent editions of their seminal work, Hawkins and Shohet added  'context' as the seventh eye in their supervisory framework.[8] We are no longer living in a changing era the theorists tell us we are living in an era of change'.[9] Twenty years ago when I began supervising, those with low morale had either lost their sense of purpose (soul) or were in the wrong job (role). With alarming regularity, I now see supervisees who are soulfully, wholehearted, committed practitioners working their socks off in roles that brought them great satisfaction in the past but which now grind them down and cause them to rethink their futures. I think of teachers who thrived in the classroom but now find themselves locked behind computer screens with endless paper work to do or residential care workers whose natural tendencies is to go the extra mile for their residents but whose wings are clipped by risk averse policies and procedures.

A 2021 British Medical Association survey found that a third of doctors are planning to retire early from the

---

[8] *Supervision in the Helping Professions,* OUP.
[9] Pope Francis is quoted as one of several who have said: 'We are not so much living in an era of change as in a change of era.' Vatican Archives, November 2015.

National Health Service after the Coronavirus pandemic, nearly a quarter are considering a career break and a fifth of younger doctors are considering quitting altogether. Long hours, high demand, the pandemic's impact, and unpleasant working environments were all cited as taking their toll on medical staff according to the survey.[10]

Attention to the context in which supervisees work takes supervision out of the traditional pastoral or therapeutic 'one on one' encounter into the sphere of organisational dysfunction, toxicity of relationships and working practices many of which are soul destroying. When I started out as a supervisor, trauma and burnout made occasional appearances in the consulting room. Now I take it as read that I am working with people whose ongoing context-induced traumas are so familiar that they barely get a mention in supervision.

'Show me the context in which you work?' can be a most revealing question for both supervisor and supervisee. Having lots of space can be helpful here as can having a wide range of materials at the supervisee's disposal.

'Let's start by finding something(s) to represent the organisation you work for. Allow yourself to rummage and choose whatever resonates with the organisation you work for. ... Now maybe you would like to add some of the people you work alongside ... And what about the dynamics in the organisation, how would it be to somehow represent them here too?'

---

[10] Quoted in *The Guardian*, 3 May 2021.

Now take a good look at what you have chosen and tell me what you notice. …

Anything else you would like to add?

Anything missing?

Are you here? If so, where do you place yourself? If not, what does that tell you?

> 'When we stop jabbering long enough to listen to what is going on around, among, and inside us – and we have someone to help us put that into the fewest, truest words available to us – the air clears and the aliveness flows through all the spaces in between.'[11]

Having someone to help us stop jabbering, having someone who can help us listen to what is going on behind the scenes, beneath the words, around, among and within us, is worth its weight in gold.

In the scenario at the start of this chapter, my mental jabberings about what I would use my breath for, were driving me round and round in circles. I needed accompanied. I needed someone to bear witness to my inner churnings. I needed someone who would not reach to fix me or worse still, answer my question for me. I needed someone who would respect my tough, resilient yet exceedingly shy soul until clarity emerged from the silence and I could 'catch a glimpse of the precious wildness' I was seeking.

---

[11] Barbara Brown Taylor cited on www.poeticmedicine.org

Creativity in supervision is not about novelty. Supervision does not chase novelty. Supervision pursues insight. For that reason, the modalities used in supervision must always take second place to the pursuit of insight. Insight and wisdom are what is being sought: modalities are the means by which we access them. Supervisors need as wide a range of modalities at their disposal as possible. There is no one size fits all. Nor should any one supervisee always be expected to work in imagery because they are visual, or in poetry because they are lyrical. Some of the most effective supervision sessions I have experienced have been with wordsmiths who tell me they won't be playing with toys and then, when words fail them, find themselves doing just that and being surprised by the results. Similarly, I have worked with people who protest that they cannot draw and then proceed to explore a complex contextual issue with a scrap of A4 and three crayons. Supervision becomes *super* when it is expansive. Supervision becomes *visionary* when people reconnect with the fire in their bellies and can spot what quickens and what threatens to extinguish that inner flame. And supervision becomes pastoral when wellbeing is extended and offered to all concerned. In the supervision session I recounted earlier, the purple flower under the palm tree was one answer to my question: 'what will I use my breath for?' The writing of this book is another.

Supervisory Space

A space filled with grace
so pervasive
that one can't help
but bump into it
and the resultant spillage
illuminates
and transforms
encounter

A space filled with light
that seeps into
every nook and cranny
that rests
in dark crevices
unfurling itself
like a cat stretching in the sun
until a different hue is detected
inviting fresh exploration
beyond the shadows

A space filled with presence
when souls show up
prepared for encounter
accompanying one another
beyond that which is visible
in the room
tapping into a wisdom
that just needed a bit of coaxing to emerge

And the acknowledgment
of the presence of God
in it all

The grace
The light
The presence
weaving it all together
making whole.

~ Liz Crumlish

Against the Tide

The wavetops rise then hang, not crashing
Until their fullest face has been revealed.

The waters tipped aside, suspended
Taut through swell and gust
From deepest sea and furthest sky.

If great impervious ocean
is not spared these cross-currents of
opposite force,
then how can I
claim exemption?

I crave the safety of alignment
But instead must walk
The wildness of the waters.

Many waters cannot quench love
Neither can the floods drown it
Love is strong as death.[12]

---

[12] This poem was written by a friend who wishes to remain anonymous.

Two vessels

Two vessels on life's journey
searching for the light.
sometimes it seems a bright star,
other times merely a flickering candle,
sometimes missed completely
in our inexperience and anxiety.
Sometimes lingering and enjoying the light and warmth
and sometimes hurrying on,
afraid of getting burnt.
But together we give each other courage
to stand in the light,
and remember our common source
and our common search.

~ Maggie Lunan

Part One
The Supervisory Relationship

Preparing to host a supervisee

I take time…
time for the place and the space;
time for me.

I shut doors…
physically shutting out the evidences of family life;
mentally shutting out the detritus of my mind.

I open up to sunlight…
and try to open myself up to the light
of Christ in my soul.

I focus on just being in His light,
open, ready, waiting…
yet at peace.

~ Frances Bloomfield

> 'The starting point for creativity is silence...
> the creative soil of silence, where can be
> found the seed-states of all things.'
>
> David Spangler, *Art: A Contemplation*

Supervisors who think that they are supervising supervisee's caseloads often take notes as aide memoires of what was brought to supervision. I propose something different. I propose that supervisors take notes, not about their supervisees nor about the content of what was explored in supervision, but about themselves: about their pre-transference[13] responses to seeing a supervisee's name in their diary and about their true feelings towards supervisees.

Noting the impact supervisees have on us, our reactions to seeing their names in our diaries calls us back to the soul of supervision. We meet to facilitate insight, not to gain reputation or approval. We meet with an eye beyond the room for the wellbeing of those with whom our supervisees work. Falling into patterns of collusion and avoidance will not serve them. I am blessed to have a number of supervisees who are a real delight to spend time with. On some days I would rather meet them for coffee and a friendly chat than occupy the role of supervisor. Being aware of this stops me from allowing

---

[13] Pre-transference is a way of speaking about thoughts, feelings, sensations which arise in the supervisor before they actually meet the supervisee. These could arise from initial contact by email or phone or as the supervisor is about to open the door or admit a supervisee to an online meeting. Pre-transference is an impactful experience which arises from the unconscious.

the supervision session to stray from its clear intention and descend into meeting my needs for good company.

I have also supervised people whose names in my diary provoke fear in me. Allowing myself to notice that I expect to be tried and tested, poked, and prodded and ultimately discarded as less than useless by the end of the session invites me to 'show up with no guarantee of the outcome'[14] rather than to be defensive and self-justifying.

Paying attention to our pre-transference thoughts, fantasies and feelings not only before we meet a new supervisee for the first time but also before meeting those we know really well can provide rich information for the session ahead. Pre-transference, which arises as 'momentary awareness' often comes 'as an unexpected visitor' to the supervisor's door. 'Welcome and entertain them all', Rumi urges, 'treat each guest honourably. The dark thought, the shame, the malice, meet them at the door laughing and invite them in.'[15]

The most important moment in supervision

Experience has led me to believe that the most important moment in supervision is the moment before we even begin. The moment of silence. Of awareness. Of clearing. Of making space inside my busy self to offer hospitality to you the one I am about to meet.

---

[14] According to Brené Brown 'vulnerability is not winning or losing; it's having the courage to show up and be seen when we have no control over the outcome.' *Rising Strong* (2015) Penguin Random House USA.
[15] Jalāl ad-Dīn Mohammad Rumi, *The Guest House*

Before meeting for the first time

What am I feeling as I enter this space?
Nervous energy, hope, excitement.
What is really going on here – am I missing something?
Leave room for God to be present!

Nervous energy, hope, excitement.
Listen; just listen.
Leave room for God to be present!
There is much more here than the spoken word –
gestures, expressions, deep feelings.

Listen; just listen.
What is really going on here – am I missing something?
There is much more here than the spoken word –
gestures, expressions, deep feelings.
What am I feeling as I enter this space?

What is really going on here – am I missing something?
Be watchful, ever watchful.
What am I feeling as I enter this space?
Your story, my story – weaving together!

Be watchful, ever watchful.
What is really going on here – am I missing something?
Your story, my story – weaving together!
What am I feeling as I enter this space?

~ Margaret Speechley

First meeting

'How are we going to be together?' is a question that needs addressing at the beginning of a new supervisory relationship. Those with no prior experience of supervision may wonder how to fill the unforgiving hour. What are they meant to talk about? Supervisees who find themselves in the room for the first time in response to some crisis in their working lives may be so bursting to share their stories that they have not given any thought whatsoever to the relationship that is about to begin. Supervisors on the other hand may be keen to start by ironing out expectations and establishing a contract that both parties can sign up to.

I have come to see contracting as more of a process than an event and would argue against introducing them in the first session. If I am thinking of buying a car, I am likely to read up about it, make inquiries about it, test drive it and only when I have a sense of what the car can do and how it suits my needs will I be ready to sign a contract and buy it. Similarly, when buying a house. I will have read the particulars. Perhaps visited the neighbourhood. Booked a viewing. Asked questions long before I sign a contract of purchase. Why is it then that so many supervisors present new supervisees with a ready-made – one size (almost) fits all contract at the first meeting? This is contracting as an event. I prefer to think of contracting as a process that takes time.

The argument against what I am proposing says that without a contract the supervisee is not offered sufficient safety and containment with which to begin. In response I would argue that presenting a supervisee with a contract – especially a ready-made one that the supervisor gives to all their supervisees – is an extraordinary display of power and falls far short of the kind of collaborative conversational relationship that invites the soul out of hiding. Sam Wells puts it very strikingly:

> 'Take contracts seriously. Care and detail over contracts is a form of love towards those we don't know very well. It's a recognition that life is full of unexpected pitfalls, and contracts are a way of holding one another to honesty and honour in the face of temptation and distraction. Contracts can give us security and trust. We should always aspire for every relationship to become a covenant, but we

should never let any relationship fall below the level of a contract.'[16]

Here is a contract aspiring to be a covenant that I often invite people to adopt just to cover us for the first hour or first few hours until we are jointly ready to co-create a contract for our work together. It is based on the Beatitudes and may be used in individual or in group supervision.

---

[16] Sam Wells, (2013) *Learning to Dream Again: Rediscovering the Heart of God, London:* Canterbury Press, 44.

Two versions are offered here. The original and a slightly adapted version.

> **A covenant for supervision**
>
> Today may I …
> Live with open hands
> Mourn what's broken
> Serve with self-respect
> Use my power for good
> Look with compassion
> Walk in honesty
> Reach past difference
> Suffer for love
> and live fearlessly
> following the way of radical love. [17]
>
> As we enter this sacred space
> May we receive each other with open hearts
> Acknowledge what is broken
> Serve with dignity
> Use power for good
> Look with compassion
> Walk in honesty
> Reach past difference
> Practice costly love
> and be courageous
> following the Way of Radical Love.

---

[17] NINE BEATS Collective / Mark Scandrette (2017), Ninefold Path Notebook, p82, published by Lifewords. With permission.

In the space between us

In the space between us,
beneath a veneer of words
behind a wall of chatter
there is...
perhaps there is something more,
emerging.

Then and there meet
here and now,
and something
bubbles up
in the texture of our sharing.

More presence than object,
defying definition
or exhibition,
Like water it escapes my grasp,
but whets
my curiosity.
Unnamed,
it feels gut-heavy.
The weight of my fear?
A burden you bear?
Named,
perhaps a doorway
to a journey into a new dimension,
immersed in depths and shapes yet unfathomed;
or perhaps a line cast fruitlessly on the waves,
less the one that got away,
more the one that never was.

It takes courage,
to cast off fear
and name this tentative something between us.
I invite you to dip your toe
in the water of possibility.

Breath baited, I wait.
And then I see you enter the water,
relax in the embrace of the deep
and swim free.

~ Diana Hall

When to introduce creativity?

Supervisors are often anxious about introducing creative modalities into their work and want to know whether it will work or not. The clues as to whether a supervisee is open to working creatively are often present in the casual chit-chat between opening the door and settling the person into the room or, when working online, as both parties establish whether they can see and hear each other and adjust their viewing options accordingly.

> 'I was worried I wouldn't find you so I came early. And then when I found the house it took me a couple of times driving around the block to find a parking space. There are some lovely old trees around here. I sat in the car just staring up at that cherry blossom in your neighbour's garden. The colours are stunning.'

A perceptive supervisor would have noticed the supervisee's attraction to visual stimuli and the natural world. At this point, seconds into the first meeting, she simply notices this and wonders whether visual stimuli might be something this supervisee could engage with in supervision. She does not presume it will be but notices that exploratory approaches which favour visual stimuli could be something this particular supervisee might well respond to.

> 'Can you see me? Can you hear me?. I've been anxious that I wouldn't get through.

This blessed Wi-Fi has been up and down all day.'

A perceptive supervisor would have picked up the supervisee's anxiety that they might not connect which has already set the tone for the session. In response the supervisor could invite the supervisee to pause and breathe before going any further. Or they could ask the supervisee to allow their eyes to scan the room and to alight on something that would support them for this session. Supervisees do not necessarily have to tell the supervisor where their eyes have landed but simply be encouraged to allow themselves to rest their focus upon it and allow it to calm them down.

Within the first meeting

One of the things that it is really helpful to find out at the first meeting are what support structures supervisees have in their lives. It makes a huge difference to the supervisory relationship to know that you are working with someone who in addition to seeing you is also seeing a counsellor for personal issues, a spiritual director for soul work and a yoga teacher for relaxation. The opposite is also true. Supervisors need to be aware of the implications of a new supervisee saying 'you are the only person I talk to'.

One of the least threatening ways to introduce creative action methods in supervision is to invite a new supervisee to use a small world collection[18] or a set of image cards to show you the support structures in their life. As they lay them down the supervisor needs to refrain from interpretation and instead, invite the supervisee to say what *they* notice, what causes *them* to wonder, what *they* realise.[19]

From that initial inquiry, the supervisor might then ask a new supervisee to choose something to represent what they are looking for from this supervisory relationship.

> 'This is what I am looking for.
>
> This is what won't work for me'.

When starting out with someone who has previous experience of supervision, the supervisor might additionally ask 'can you show me how it is to meet a new supervisor for the first time?' A supervisor could follow this up by choosing an object or image card which expresses their own feelings about this new beginning.

---

[18] Mooli Lahad coined this term for sculpting in miniature. (2000) *Creative Supervision: The Use of Expressive Arts in Supervision and Self Supervision*, London: Jessica Kingsley

[19] The three levels of seeing of Contemplative Inquiry, see Leach and Paterson(2015) *Pastoral Supervision: A Handbook*, 63-7.

A recognition of what I bring to what others bring

Newly laid turf
An apparently seamless carpet of green
'Water it frequently', I'm told
Hose in hand, my eye alights on some bare patches
I spend longer here
Then, spotting the cracks where squares don't quite meet
Directing the nozzle at the narrow channels between,
Trusting, in time, the edges somehow will connect,
Forming a whole

From a distance, all looked well, complete
Close up I engage consciously with the not-so-fine,
Areas I see needing extra attention, more care
These my focus, rather than what is already, quietly, flourishing

I think about my life
My tendency to highlight its bare patches and cracks –
Genuine or perceived
A reticence to nourish, affirm, celebrate the positive

And, as a supervisor,
With supervisees (and peers),
My inner critic's 'attraction' to 'problems',
Operating from a deficit model
Slow to acknowledge what's good,
To nurture and encourage,
To be fully open and hospitable -
Realising I want to offer more space . . . more grace,
To others . . . and to me
~ Joyce Wintour

When the unconscious presents its calling card

In his wonderful book *The Boy, the Fox, the Mole and the Horse*, Charlie Mackesy has a wonderful drawing of the boy gazing into a puddle and seeing his own reflection in the water. 'Isn't it odd' the caption says, 'we can only see our outsides, but nearly everything happens on the inside.'

The unconscious is always present in supervision. Sometimes its presence is welcomed and embraced. Sometimes it shows up unexpectedly causing alarm and disturbing things. Howsoever it manifests, the unconscious is always information: information about what is not being said, information about some thought or feeling which is not being owned, information about some dynamic which resists being named and brought into the light, information about some unresolved story which is being rehearsed again and again.

Hawkins and Shohet[20] talk of the then and there of the supervisee's work being played out in the here and now of the supervisory space. They identify seven eyes through which the supervisor gains different views of what is happening in the supervisee's interaction with their clients.

---

[20] *Supervision in the Helping Professions*, 5th edition Hawkins and McMahon.

The Seven Eyes

Eyes 1-3 focus on the practitioner-client realm

Eye 1: Paint me a picture of what happened when you met;

Eye 2 Show me the strategies and interventions you used;

Eye 3 Show me the relationship between your client and those involved in the situation

Eyes 4-6 focus on the practitioner-supervisor realm and explore what happens in the supervisor-supervisee relationship.

Eye 4: Show me your true feelings about the person(s) you were trying to support in your there and then story

Eye 5: What is being replayed here between the two of us (supervisor-supervisee) in the here and now that informs us about the there and then

Eye 6: In what ways is the supervisee nudging the supervisor to attend to things in their own life which are triggered by what is being explored by the supervisee

Eye 7 focuses on the context and its impact

Hawkins & Shohet

The Seven Eyes

The then and there,
two buds
of possible exploration
of a practitioner's experience.

The what and who and wherefore.
content – what happened?
The strategies and interventions;
bringing the work into the room
in the memory and relating of what was said and done.
The feel of it..
The relationship between practitioner and client
Into the space of deeper reflection.

The Here and Now
the impact of the client on the practitioner
...wondering..
Closer in,
the space between
supervisee and supervisor,
something different happening,
the possibility
of supervisee and supervisor being in parallel process

Listening to more than the story,
attuned to the scent,
aware of the impact on me
What has been stirred in me?
What do I do with this?
When and where?
A thing of beauty.
~ Helen Kearins

How much of me should show up?

The question is often asked: how do I leave myself outside the door when I go into the supervision room to accompany my supervisees? Underlying the question is a good intention: to give centre stage to the supervisee, nevertheless the question leaves me deeply saddened. If supervision is relational then why would the supervisor leave themselves outside the room? If supervision is hospitable, how hospitable is a distant supervisor who keeps people at arm's length? Hospitality requires supervisors to show up, not to stand on the lintel and peer in from a distance, but to show up, allow themselves to be seen and to sense, touch and feel the impact of those they accompany.

Showing up does not mean taking centre stage. It means being committed enough to cross the threshold 'with no guarantee of the outcome.'[21] Those who argue that supervisors should leave themselves outside the room often say that bringing anything less than objective disinterest into the room contaminates the space. I hold that effective supervision requires supervisors to become, not more objective, but more subjective. What I am arguing for is 'the intentional use of self' in the service of others. After years of tussling over objectivity and subjectivity in supervision I wrote this poem to try and undo what had been handed down to me under the guise of professional wisdom.

---

[21] 'Vulnerability is not winning or losing; it's having the courage to show up and be seen when we have no control over the outcome.' Brené Brown, *Rising Strong: How the Ability to Reset Transforms the Way We Live, Love, Parent, and Lead.*

When ALL of me

mindfully present, recollected and ready

turns up for YOU

by creating a hospitable space within me for you

then I can afford to trust that whatever happens between us

no matter how random, no matter how off the wall, may be of use to you.

Whereas when I am not present to myself

through distraction or mindlessness

and don't make space for you

by filling the space with my own insecurities fears, or need for validation

then my subjectivity

whatever happens within my head, heart, soul or body

as you speak and explore within the session

is likely to trip me up and hinder you

because I have no way of knowing if

that strange thought, that knot in my stomach,

that fleeting image that popped into my head

arises from you or from me.[22]

---

[22] This is my summary of what I understand to lie at the heart of Hawkins & Shohet's Eyes 4-6.

Reviewing the relationship

In the earlier pages of this book, I encouraged supervisors to think of contracting or covenanting more as a process than an event, something which is incremental and happens over time rather than at the first meeting. The same holds for reviewing. Why wait for things to go wrong to review the relationship?

Built into every supervisory relationship are a series of punctuation marks; the end of the first session; the review point four to six sessions in; holiday breaks; unplanned for absences, sickness, cancellations etc.

Beginning the relationship by asking what the supervisee is looking for allows the review question 'are you finding what you came for?' to be asked at the end of the first hour or block of hours.

Asking 'how will we know if this is working?' offers a point of reference to which both parties can return at any time.

Inviting a supervisee to name or show what they found helpful in previous supervision and what less so also offers something to gauge how supervisors are faring.

And having the courage to ask a supervisee at the end of a session or series of sessions, what they would like more or less of from supervision fosters practitioner autonomy, models the collaborative nature of the relationship and offers the supervisor invaluable insights into how best to adjust their approach to best meet the supervisee's needs. After all, what is hospitality if everyone is treated in the same way? If we would not think of serving a vegetarian a steak, why would we be any less hospitable in serving someone with a rich imaginative visual processing style, word based supervision.

> **Reviewing in Supervision**
>
> Show me how you are experiencing our relationship using these cards or this small world collection
>
> What metaphors would you use to describe how it is to bring your work here for supervision?
>
> If this relationship were a novel, what would its title be?
>
> If this relationship was a soap opera, what do you think would happen?
>
> If you and I were stuck on a desert island without a lifeboat or a means of escape, what do you think would happen?[23]
>
> I wonder before we next meet if you would like to paint a picture depicting the highlights and the lowlights of this relationship. (At the next meeting ask the person to tear or cut each image into strips and then weave the highlights and the lowlights together. What do you see now? What do you notice? What do you realise?

---

[23] One of the wonderfully illuminating questions that Hawkins and Shohet pose to access Eye 4 in their Seven Eyed framework.

Power and Vulnerability

reflecting on the story of the woman caught in adultery
John 8:2-11

Thrust into his space
with no formal contract
but with clear expectations:
Condemnation - the only conceivable outcome
in the eyes of the Scribes and Pharisees
But not in the alternative kingdom
which Jesus modelled
In the space where he taught
and held folk to account
to live out Scripture
He freed the woman caught in adultery
and freed the Scribes and Pharisees
from their self-righteousness.
He drew a line in the sand
and then straightened up,
looked the woman in the eye
and set her free
from condemnation
from vulnerability
from the powerful
whose power diminished
in the face of truth
and integrity
and compassion.
In the face of such subversion
we are called
to lay down our stones
and to open our hearts

to be vulnerable
with the other,
holding the space
where power and vulnerability
can be exchanged
as one ministers to the other,
as we give ourselves
and in the giving
find healing
and forgiveness
and newness of life.

~ Liz Crumlish

Unicycling Juggler

Trusting my competence
to stay upright and keep pedalling,
you throw the first idea,
watching to see what I will do with it.
then slowly – or quickly more and more
back and forth between us

I receive each word, each
nuance, each move
I focus on not dropping,
not choosing, not
rejecting, not interjecting
as I balance on a wire
(my/your power; my/your
vulnerability)
holding and releasing
noticing, wondering…

You may perceive –
despite my vulnerability and precarious juggling –
a sense of order
a joy in the experience
as noticing and wondering enable
insight, realisation, ideas and actions

Trusting your competence -
your insights, your 'aha', your power
I hand back what you have offered,
allowing you to decide, 'what next...
where will I go from here?'

~ Poem by Catriona Gorton
Images © Ljupco | Dreamstime.com

When things go wrong

Supervision, like all human relationships, does not proceed in a linear direction nor is it immune to bumps in the road. Even when time has been taken to co-create a covenant for working together, things happen which challenge trust. A cancellation at short notice on the part of the supervisor or a prolonged sickness may be experienced anywhere on a spectrum from disappointment through feeling let down to the trauma of utter abandonment. Add into the mix that the relationship is founded on a commitment to sustained dialogue between soul, role and context and the stakes mount even higher as the investment required for such explorations is deep.

Michael Carroll compares supervisory agreements to icebergs. He writes:

> 'Psychological contracts are much more prevalent than overt, negotiated, agreed contracts ... contracts are like icebergs with the formal, agreed and overt contract as the part of the iceberg that is above water, while the unseen, unnegotiated psychological contract is the part beneath water ... in our heads we work out an agreement with someone else ... unsuspectingly, we make them mentally sign it and thereafter it has all the force of a binding agreement ... it is often the difficulties in the psychological contract that results in ethical charges, formal and informal complaints, legal

stances and breakdown in professional (and indeed personal) relationships.'[24]

I have experienced breakdown in the supervisory relationship both as supervisor and supervisee.

As supervisee, one supervisor brought the relationship to an unplanned end when I shared a dream I had about her sick mother. It turned out my supervisor was estranged from her mother who was indeed sick and dying. Rather than deal with the unconscious breaking through in supervision I was cast adrift on the high seas without warning.

Another supervisor broke off our relationship because she wanted me to bring cases that she could manage by proxy and was not interested in my soul, role and context explorations.

As a supervisee I brought a relationship to an end out of exasperation over being regularly asked to spend forty minutes of a fifty minute session helping my supervisor understand things which I already understood leaving me only ten minutes to pursue the kinds of insight for which I had come.

And as a supervisor, relationships have ended because I have failed supervisees. Enraged them. Corroded their trust. Left them feeling unsafe. Misunderstood them. Taken them beyond their comfort zone without their consent. Missed the cues and warning signs they were

---

[24] Michael Carroll in Morrissey ed (2005) *Handbook of Professional & Ethical Practice for Psychologists, Counsellors and Psychotherapists*, Brunner-Routledge, 93-4.

offering me. Colluding with them by not challenging enough. Presuming more robustness than was the case. Put some off supervision altogether. Proven that men cannot be trusted. The list goes on. None of it was intended but the wounds caused are great and, in some cases, ongoing.

John O'Donohue's poem 'For the break-up of a relationship' has a lot to say to supervisors when relationships go wrong:

> Try, as best you can, not to let,
> the wire brush of doubt
> scrape from your heart
> all sense of yourself
> and your hesitant light.
>
> If you remain generous,
> time will come good;
> and you will find your feet
> again on fresh pastures of promise,
> where the air will be kind
> and blushed with beginning.[25]

---

[25] John O'Donohue (2007) *Benedictus: A Book of Blessings*, London: Bantam Press.

Endings in supervision[26]

After years of working as a chaplain in palliative care, I concur with the American physician Ira Byock[27] who writes that good endings are those in which a person has the chance to say four things:

Endings in Supervision

Thank you

I'm sorry

I release you from the past

I wish you well for the future

In my experience some people find it harder to say 'hello' in supervision and never really invest in the relationship while others find it harder to say 'goodbye' and linger at the edges and never quite leave.

Some endings are like Velcro, in which one party sticks to the other and will not let go. Some are so loose or casual that there is little evidence an

---

[26] I am indebted to Mogs Bazeley of the Institute of Pastoral Counselling & Supervision for the wonderful illustrations in this section www.pastoralcs.org.uk
[27] Ira Byock (2014) *The Four Things That Matter Most* 10th Anniversary Edition, New York: Simon and Schuster.

ending has actually taken place. 'Well, I'm sure I'll see you around'.

Some endings have all the hallmarks of grief with one or other party feeling a void open within them.

Cut and run endings are those in which supervisees cannot make the final meeting or the one after that and simply disappear without trace. Their close cousin 'bin bag' endings are those endings in which the relationship seems to be dumped in a black plastic bag like garbage as if the relationship had no value whatsoever.

Good endings in supervision are those which have been mutually negotiated rather than sprung on one party by the other. With sufficient planning, time can then be set aside to name what has been shared and experienced, the good and the bad.

Good endings are also proportionate to the relationship, the context, and the person(s) involved. Ending a four-week supervisory relationship with a student on placement may feel very different from ending a relationship with someone you have accompanied for a decade and who is now retiring.

Byock's invitation to say thank needs to be taken up on both sides. Supervisors who are at home in their own skin are able to name what supervisees have taught them and how the work has nudged them along in their own process as persons and practitioners.[28]

Once again, the hints of how the ultimate ending is likely to be experienced will have been given along the way in the micro endings of each session. Supervisees who struggle to last the hour may struggle to actually show up to say goodbye. Supervisees who linger at the door, holding you hostage at the end of a session as they launch into yet another story, may struggle to say goodbye no matter how clear supervisors are about endings.

Supervisors should be mindful that their handling of endings within the supervisory relationship will model – for good or for bad – how supervisees might handle endings in their working relationships. All the more reason then, to ensure that goodbye means goodbye and that the ending is not fudged or avoided or ambiguous.

---

[28] Hawkins and Shohet, Eye 6

Part Two
The Supervisory Process

Contemplative Inquiry
(Three Levels of Seeing)

I see, I notice, I wonder

I see,
I gaze, I take a long hard loving look
not rushing on to the next thing
but pausing long enough to behold

I wonder
I allow curiosity to slow me down,
I turn things over in my mind
I look from different angles
I allow my seeing and thinking to playfully expand

I realise
The penny drops, The pieces come together
insight is found

What do *you* see?
What do *you* wonder?
What do *you* realise?[29]

~ Michael Paterson

---

[29] These are the three verbs translated as 'seeing' in the Greek of the Resurrection account in John 20, For a fuller exploration of the three levels of seeing in supervision see Leach & Paterson, (2015) *Pastoral Supervision: A Handbook* 63-67.

Supervision invites us to take a long, hard, loving look at some aspect of our work which calls for our attention.

Three Levels of Seeing

I notice

The first level of seeing 'looking and noticing' is about observation without interpretation.

Regarded as lacking sophistication by supervisors who want to appear wise, it is often rejected.

Supervisors do this at their peril since what is obvious to one may be significant to another.

I wonder

The second level of seeing 'wondering' is about allowing our curiosity to run freely.

How else could this be seen?

What else could this mean?

If these things could speak what might they say?

I realise

The third level of seeing is that moment when the penny drops and things fall into place.

It is the moment of insight and of perception.

The three levels of seeing are used in supervision to slow things down and open up an expansive space for reflection. They are also used to save the supervisee from being interpreted by the supervisor. Noticing allows the ordinary not to be overlooked. Wondering allows tentative inquiry, which in the spirit of hospitality, leaves the supervisee free to buy into the wondering or reject it. And realising holds out for insight, that 'aha' moment in which inquiry is met with recognition.

Contemplative inquiry enables supervisees to hone the material they present in supervision by slowing down the pace.

> 'I noticed that you told that story in one great big whoosh, hardly pausing to come up for breath'.
>
> 'I hadn't realised that but you are right, that is how it feels. No breathing space just about sums it up.'

Contemplative inquiry prioritises what the supervisee sees, wonders or realizes over the supervisor's interpretations. So, for example when a supervisee represents the issue they are bringing to supervision using objects or image cards the first response from the supervisor should be 'what do you see as you look?' rather than 'I can tell that ...'

In the same vein, supervisors are cautioned against taking things at face value. The objects or images or story lines a supervisee chooses in supervision may have quite different meanings for them than they do for the supervisor. Example: in response to the question, 'could you show me the team you work with?, a supervisee might place a series of stones on the floor. To the supervisor these could look like hard, inanimate, impermeable objects. To the supervisee, however, they might mean solid, reliable, wizened by age qualities. Asking supervisees what they notice in what they have chosen, or wondering whether perception changes by turning the chosen objects around or by moving out of their chairs to see the representation from a different angle facilitates the supervisee's internal exploration and protects them from becoming entangled in the supervisor's interests or processes.

It is of course perfectly legitimate and appropriate for supervisors to offer what they notice or wonder but only after the supervisee has spoken first.

> I noticed that you said your colleagues were solid and reliable.
>
> I wonder if you could choose something to represent you among your colleagues.

and after they have placed themselves

> I wonder what you see now?

Noticing, wondering, and realising can also be used to name dynamics in the supervisory relationship. For example

> You are speaking about the pressure you feel to solve this for your team. But the more you talk, the more I notice the pressure I feel to help you find a solution.
>
> I notice that your urgency to resolve this has filled the space between us.
>
> I realise that we have spent the last fifteen minutes in problem solving mode. I wonder what it would take to slow things down and reflect rather than react....
>
> I wonder whose role it is to resolve this?

Contemplative Inquiry. Noticing, wondering, realizing. Three verbs. Three forms of facilitating space. Three correctives to clever analysis or interpretation.

Repeated research has shown that the single most important factor in facilitating wellbeing (whether in pastoral care, counselling, supervision etc) is the quality of the relationship between the participants. Listening is fundamental to that relationship. Nancy Kline[30] identifies three different kinds of listening each of which can feature in supervision.

---

[30] Nancy Kline, (1999) *Time to Think,* London: Cassell. See too Nancy Kline (2020) *The promise that changes everything: I won't interrupt you'* London: Penguin.

Three kinds of Listening

I interrupt, I understand, I ignite

I interrupt,
eager to guide you
support you,
inform you.
I interrupt,
keen to have something to say.
I interrupt,
you lose heart.

I understand
I want to know the facts
I want to know the details
I want to piece it all together.
I now know what you knew already.
Nothing has changed.
You lose interest.
You lose heart.

I ignite
I catch your spark.
I feel your heat.
I warm to your passion.
I extinguish
I smell the smoke.
I see the ashes.
I mourn your loss.

~ Michael Paterson

Listening to Interrupt

This is when the supervisor is not so much listening to the supervisee as looking for every opportunity to get their tuppence worth into the conversation. Underlying 'listening to interrupt' is the presumption that the supervisor knows best.

Listening to interrupt is most likely to be present when supervisor/supervisee are working within the same discipline (teacher with a teacher for example) and when the supervisor is more senior to the supervisee. At best, the result of such a conversation is information exchange. At worst, the supervisor seeks self-validation but leaves the supervisee feeling diminished. Caring supervisors can indulge in listening to interrupt when they fill the supervisory space with their own anxieties or act under pressure to prove themselves. Listening to interrupt can also happen when supervisors confuse empathic resonance *with* their supervisees for an urgency to fix things *for* them.

Listening to Understand

This kind of listening happens when supervisors act on the mistaken belief that the more they understand their supervisees' issues, the more helpful they will be. This results in supervisors working hard to understand what supervisees are presenting and supervisees working hard to make themselves understood.

The positive effect of this kind of listening is that supervisees may feel the empathy and genuine care of their supervisors. The downside is that supervisees often have to spend more time than they would like in the session helping supervisors understand things that are already deeply familiar to them. To supervisors this can be very informative as they get a sense of how things fit together. To supervisees, however, this can be tedious and frustrating since it keeps the supervisory session in the realms of what is known rather than in the pursuit of something new and energising. Supervisors who *listen to understand* make good use of tracking, paraphrasing, and summarising what supervisees say. Transformation, however, is more likely to occur when supervisees are invited to track their own use of language, metaphor, energy, and interest.

Listening to Ignite

Listening to ignite happens when both parties go into the supervisory space with curiosity and open themselves up to whatever may emerge in the conversation. This kind of supervisory conversation does not require supervisors to have any idea whatsoever what supervisees are talking about. Listening to ignite invites supervisors to follow supervisees interests, energies, passions and vision as they wax and wane in the session.

Listening to ignite fundamentally re-connects supervisees to their 'why'. In creative supervision, listening for what ignites and what extinguishes supervisees releases supervisors from having to understand the movements supervisees make or the small world objects they choose in exploring their supervisory questions. Freed from pursuing understanding, supervisors become available to facilitate supervisee's internal processes by asking questions such as:

- What strikes you in the images you have chosen?
- Where does that piece of music take you?
- How does what we are exploring sit with your values?
- Where are we now?

> Listening to interrupt leads to information exchange.
>
> Listening to understand leads to re-formation of ideas and shared understanding .
>
> Listening to ignite leads to transformation and to re-connection with personal motivation.[31]

---

[31] Bobby Moore (2016) *Reflexive Supervision*, 67-72.

The Supervisory Process

Setting up
You cleared the space
lined up the tripod (checking the legs for wobbles)
cleaned the lens of the telescope
filled the kettle, the fridge and the biscuit tin
and you waited for me

Settling
You settled me:
'comfied me in' with a cuppa and a cushion
listened for my breath and allowed yours to match
until we were apace with one another
whatever the pace was on that day
you pointed out some stuff that might help me
during our time together
and you welcomed me

Searching
And then you sat next to me
as I looked to the night sky
you didn't judge me as I struggled to focus the lens
sometimes desperately wanting to see something that
just wasn't there
sometimes frustrated by the fog
and you watched with me

Sifting
And you sifted as I found one star then another
a meteor, some lightning
a constellation
until I zoomed in and out and in again of the biggest
bit of my sky on that day

Noticing the detail
and you helped me to peel away the layer of shame I
came prepared to pop over my lens
so that I could bear looking more closely at the picture
exploring what would happen if I were to dance in it,
shout at it, run round it,
and you wondered with me

Shifting
And you shifted gears with me
when I decided what I would do
when I mapped my course
and whistled my own tune in response to that piece of
my sky
and you whistled my tune back to me to make sure
you'd heard it right

Sending
You gave me space to capture the notes
to let my rhythm settle enough in me
before
helping me re-notice the breathing of 'out there'
and then you encouraged me to go back
equipped with my tune and our plan to meet again
and you waved to me

So now to me....
Setting up
I clear the space
line up the tripod (checking the legs for wobbles)
clean the lens of the telescope
fill the kettle, the fridge and the biscuit tin
and I wait....
~ Ali Pandian

As an intentional space, supervision has a clear structure characterised by six processes.[32]

> **The Supervision Sat Nav**
>
> *Hosting and Containing*
>
> focuses on the kind of hospitality which enables transformative learning. This includes attention to the ethical framework, organization culture, immediate environment, and quality of interpersonal relationship between participants.
>
> *Eliciting and Focusing*
>
> is not only about getting the work into the room but about identifying the energy or impulse that will make reflection worthwhile, i.e. What is it in particular about this that makes it worth looking at here today?

---

[32] This six process approach is explored in-depth in Paterson (2020) *Between a Rock and a Hard Place: Pastoral Supervision Revisited and Revisioned,* Edinburgh: IPSRP, Chapter Seven

Exploring and Imagining.

Once a focus has been established, exploring and imagining becomes a playful and creatively fertile place in which to try out ideas and ways of working. It is also the place in which stray thoughts, fantasies, images and metaphors can be aired.

Tracking and Monitoring.

Tracking is both a discreet moment in the reflective cycle and something that runs through the whole session. It is a way of monitoring that what is happening is matching what it is needed within the allotted time.

Bridging and Enacting

are reminders that we reflect on work from the *past*, in the *present* in order to change and enhance work in the *future*. A bridge is built out from the reflective time and back into the world of everyday practice. Enacting names the first steps to be taken.

Reviewing and Closing

is the process of naming what has been learned through reflection and the drawing of a line on the exploration. In supervision, closing well is just as important as beginning well.

Each of these processes will be explored in this section with practical suggestions offered for using creative modalities in each.

Hosting & Containing

After two decades of supervising, the word that best sums supervision up for me is hospitality: hospitality towards each other; hospitality towards the material that is brought; hospitality towards the strange or surprising insights that emerge; hospitality to the modalities used for exploration and hospitality towards the process. Without hospitality the time is likely to be transactional: I (supervisee) bring material that you (supervisor) pore over. Hospitality in supervision makes the time relational: I (supervisee) co-create a space with you (supervisor) in which we explore my work.

Hospitality has connotations of homeliness, of calm environments where needs are catered for. When someone is coming to dinner, hospitality requires us to prepare: to shop, to cook, to set the table. We do all these things so that the guest feels welcome and enjoys their time with us. So too hospitality in supervision begins with preparation, those things which make it possible for the other to feel welcome.

When meeting face to face we pay attention to the physical environment in which we will have our session. We attend to the lighting, the heating. We have a chair or cushion or floor space ready. We have our creative toolkits at hand in case we may require them.

Attention to hospitality is every bit as important when meeting on digital platforms. What background am I showing? Does the space behind me suggest busyness or calm, spaciousness, or clutter? And is the space behind me mine to show or am I disclosing things about my family, house mates or colleagues which is not mine to broadcast?

And what about inner hospitality? The outer space needs to be matched by an inner spaciousness that the supervisor creates in which to welcome and make room for the supervisee. I have come to believe that moments before supervision actually begins – the moment before the door or phone rings or the Zoom call comes through – are the most important moments in supervision and that those moments of stilling ourselves to offer inner hospitality to the other saves us hours of rambling false starts in supervision.

Ways of offering hospitality

There are many ways of finding hospitality for those you about to meet.

Breathing Exercise

Take some deep breaths. On the outbreath, let go of what you have been doing for now. On the inbreath, make room to welcome the person you are about to meet.

Continue to breathe out anything that would get in the way of being fully present with that person.

Breathe in the courage, the presence, the commitment to meet them as they are.

Once seated with the person (or once connected online) you might like to invite the supervisee to take the time to come into this space and time. Rather than second guessing what works for your supervisee foster their autonomy and ask them how they would like to begin. Here are some options:

Ways of Beginning

Take a moment to settle yourself while I get you a glass of water.

Settle into the chair and become aware of your surroundings.

Pause for a moment and, when you are ready to begin, light a candle.

Take off your shoes when you are ready to begin.

Take a moment to allow yourself to arrive. I won't speak until you tell me you are ready.

Pick up a stone representing whatever you are carrying today that will not serve you in this session. And then when you are ready, put that stone down by the door, ready to be picked up after our session.

Allow your eye to scan the room, and let it rest on something which could support you for the next hour.

Beginning with a Group

Ask 'What would get in the way of you being here right now?'

Supervisor places a large box in the middle of the room

I now invite you to place all those things which are important but would get in the way of you being fully present here with each other today into this box.

I promise to keep those things safe till later.

Supervisor carefully wraps the box in a cloth/or ties it in a ribbon.

I am going to place the box by the door so that you can collect what you need as you leave today.

And now, having laid aside those things aside, ask yourself what would help and support you to be here right now?

Become aware of all that would support you to be here today.

It is yours and no-one can take it away from you.

And so let us begin…

Eliciting and Focusing

Sometimes people know exactly what they want to explore in supervision and dive straight in while supervisors listen and watch from the side lines trying to catch up. Sometimes supervisees do not have a clue what to bring and a silence descends like a mist over the supervision room. Anxious supervisors, sensing the awkwardness of the silence may be tempted to play the role of rescuer and too easily run with any space filler that supervisees offer rather than do the harder work of eliciting something that really matters. I am not suggesting that people should always bring big issues or dramas, but I am arguing that whatever is brought has to hold within it some charge or frisson for the supervisee; something that is itchy in the supervisee's practice; something which is live and real. Supervisees should be discouraged from bringing already worked out scenarios which they have done to death by prior thinking or consultation. Fresh, raw, in the moment realities are the meat and drink of supervision.

Supervisors need also be mindful that those unfamiliar with supervision may easily mistake reporting for reflecting. If the supervisor needs a report, she must say so otherwise reporting should be consigned to the line management relationship, leaving the supervisory space open for reflection, exploration and imaginative discovery. Language is crucial. A supervisor who begins by asking 'what would you like to discuss today?' has only themselves to blame when a generalised conversation about some topic or other distracts both parties from the real task of reflection on practice.

'Which aspect of your work would you like to reflect on today?' is a more focused and appropriate question.

But I just don't know what to look at today

Sometimes supervisees struggle to choose where to focus because in choosing to look at issues A, B and C they will not have a chance to look at issues X, Y and Z. Helping people narrow choices down at the beginning of a session will save a lot of time later. Here are some ways of eliciting and focusing:

> Which aspect of your work would you like to explore here today?
>
> When you think of all the things that have happened at work since we last met which of them still have resonance for you?
>
> What would be a good use of time today?
>
> Using these image cards could you show me your month in pictures …. What do you realise from your choice of images?
>
> I wonder how your soul and role have been getting on in your context since we last met?
>
> If the last month at work was a soap opera what would it be called?
>
> If you were to tweet the highs and lows of the time interval since we last met, what would those tweets say?

Exploring & Imagining

Having elicited a focus for the session, the stage is now set for the chief work of the session which is exploration. Asking 'what would you like to *explore* today?' sets the tone for something provisional, adventurous, and as yet unknown. But there is more since the story brought is often not in fact the real issue but rather the bearer of the issue.

> 'I want to look at my anxieties about my fortnightly shift in the dementia care unit.'

Two questions immediately arise in response to what has been named

> 'Would you like to talk about it or would you like to explore it in some other way?'

By asking *how* the supervisee would like to explore their issue, supervisors implicitly underscore the hospitality they are offering in making themselves available to facilitate the supervisee's process.

> 'I would like to talk about it.'

Being directed by the supervisee towards a verbal modality opens up a whole range of possibilities:

> 'Where would you like to begin?'

Notice how different that question is from a supervisor saying 'how long have you been anxious'. The latter shapes the interaction according to the supervisor's interest. The former says to the supervisee 'I am interested in whatever it is about this that interests you'.

Continuing with a verbal modality, the supervisor could ask the supervisee to say what size the anxiety is? ... What shape it is? Or where they feel it in their body? etc

If a supervisee indicates that they are open to exploring their issue in ways which are not only verbal the supervisor could invite the supervisee to

> Swap roles with their anxiety and hear what it has to say.[33]
>
> Engage in a two-way conversation with their anxiety.
>
> Choose an object to represent their anxiety.
>
> Choose a place in the room to position that representation of anxiety and then take up a physical position as near or as far as they wish to that object

In all of these examples, asking the supervisee what they noticed, wondered or realised (contemplative inquiry) before saying what you, the supervisor notice, wonder or realise will be more impactful and will offer the supervisor invaluable guidance as to where to focus their attention in facilitating the supervisee's search for insight.

---

[33] See Anna Chesner 'Role as a key concept in supervision' in Chesner and Zografou, (2014) Creative Supervision across Modalities, London: Jessica Kingsley, 43-57.

Tracking & Monitoring

There is a popular greeting card which depicts a man and his wife clothed in Victorian dress standing beside a Penny Farthing with the caption: 'Thanks to the Sat Nav we can now get lost much more accurately'.

The supervisory process – the Sat Nav I have indicated - certainly does not guarantee you from ever getting lost. What it does do, however, is help the lost supervisor get back on the road again after the wrong turns or blind alleys that ensue in supervision. Nor is the supervisory Sat Nav simply sequential. While it is true that hosting and containing are given particular attention at the beginning of the session, hospitality continues as an ethos which permeates the entire supervisory space from beginning to end. Similarly, while eliciting and focusing provide the launching pad for exploration, deeper levels of focus emerge throughout as the exploration becomes more finely tuned and nuanced. It is not unusual for a supervisee to say twenty or thirty minutes into a session: 'I thought, when I started, the issue was X, but I now realise it's actually Y'.

Tracking and monitoring have various dimensions: tracking the time; ascertaining whether the exploration is helpful to the supervisee or not; monitoring the effectiveness of the modality being used; tracking whether the approach taken results in complexifying or simplifying the issue being explored.

Supervisors who have been trained in listening techniques frequently take the burden of tracking upon themselves. 'You said you wanted to look at X, and then you realised it was Y and now you seem to be saying Z.'

I take the view that supervisors should notice all those things and even wonder about them but should keep those noticings and wonderings (at least initially) to themselves. They form part of the attentive hospitality that supervisors pay supervisees, but they also run the huge risk of supervisors prioritising their own interests, interpretations or need to be helpful over supervisees' needs to be accompanied. Experience has taught me that, time and time again, insight arises mostly from supervisees tracking themselves.

Tracking & Monitoring

Of all the things you have heard yourself say, what sticks with you right now?

Of the feelings that have arisen as you have explored this issue, what has been uppermost?

Where are you now?

Creative modalities can be used to answer these questions in non-verbal ways.

> **Creative Tracking & Monitoring**
>
> I wonder if you could choose something to indicate where you are now with the issue?
>
> I wonder what in this room conveys where you are at this stage of our exploration? (carpet, curtains, chairs, cushions, artwork on walls etc)
>
> If you were to give this exploration a title, what would it be?
>
> I wonder if you could express what you are finding in your body through adopting a posture or a series of movements?

Bridging & Enacting

The whole purpose of supervision is summed up in Donald Schön's dictum: 'We reflect on the past, in the present for the sake of the future.'[34] If supervision only reflects on the past with no attention to the future, then it is a form of creative or linguistic archaeology which expends its energies pouring over the artefacts of practice. And if supervision only reflects on the past in the present then it may be accusatory and blaming, or analytical and

---

[34] Donald Schön (1985) *The Reflective Practitioner*

detached. Worse still it may simply be a moan fest. 'Start with the end in mind', urges Steve Covey.[35] Supervision is not an end in itself, far less a matter of compliance. Supervision has an agenda about which it is utterly transparent and unashamed. We reflect on the past in the present for the sake of a better future. A better future for supervisees for sure, but ultimately a better future for those in their care and for the organisations in which they operate. And here we come full circle to our earlier discussion of supervision as the facilitated, intentional, and accompanied conversation between soul, role and context. Systemic wellbeing is the name of the game. Systemic wellbeing is the end to which supervision is directed.

Building a bridge from reflecting on practice in supervision (the past) to enacting whatever insights have been found in the workplace (future) requires explicit attention in the present.

What will you do (when back at work) with what you have found here today (in supervision)?

What might help you remember the insight you found here?

How could you hold onto your new thinking or understanding when you go from here today?

---

[35] Steve Covey, (1990) *Seven Habits of Highly Effective People*, New York: Simon and Shuster.

For visual processors, choosing a slogan or an image, an internalised source of wisdom or a moment in a story can help them encapsulate their new found insight. Some examples of non-verbal bridging:

> I am going to put a photo of my gran on my laptop so that next time I am on zoom with X, I can look at her and remember that she believed in me and feel her support.
>
> I am going home to watch the Lion King again. I think that scene where Simba is talking to Rafiki is what I need to revisit.
>
> I am going to take a photo of the small world installation I made today and put it on my computer as a screen saver for a week or so.

Gloria Anzaldúa writes:

> On the path ahead you see a footbridge with missing planks, broken rails. You walk toward it, step onto the threshold and freeze, right hand clutching the past, left hand stretching toward the unknown. Behind, the world admonishes you to stick to the old-and-tried ways, and the securities they offer. But 'Go!', says your inner spirit, 'you have a calling' and 'only you can bring forth your potential'.[36]

---

[36] Gloria Anzaldúa, *Borderlands*, 1987. Gloria lived her whole life in the in-between places of geography, race, language, colour,

Supervision offers a bridge from insight on one side to enactment on the other. Crossing the bridge takes courage. Returning to the 'same old, same old' is much easier. But transformation is impatient and pushes for an answer. Will you, or won't you? Supervisors have a key role to play as cheerleaders and eager supporters lending everything we have to convey the message: 'You can do it. I've got your back!'

Reviewing & Closing

When a friend comes to dinner, no decent host would be standing there, coat in hand, as they downed the last morsel of food, ushering them out the door. Such behaviour would be experienced as rude and would undermine the whole experience of the evening. So too, hospitality requires as much care as the supervision session comes to an end as it does at the beginning. Leaving time for the exchanges that come with saying goodbye are just as important whether meeting in person or online.

Practicalities at this stage may include fixing a date and time in the diary for the next meeting; finding that book or article you promised to lend the supervisee during the session; receiving payment etc. Factoring all this in by working backwards from the agreed finishing time is all part of tracking and monitoring.

If due care and attention has been taken to elicit a focus and to track emerging insight within the session, then

---

belief and sexuality. She was born and raise on the Texas/Mexico border. Crossing bridges was her life's work.

only a few minutes will typically be required for reviewing and closing. If, however, the supervisee has touched into a deep level of emotional, psychological, or spiritual distress, then a much longer time may need to be allocated to reviewing and closing to ensure that the supervisee is in a sufficiently healthy state to drive home or go back to work. One side effect of working online is that some supervisees, finding themselves in the safety and security of their own homes, go far deeper in their soul, role, context explorations than they allowed themselves when meeting their supervisors in person. The transition from being accompanied during the session to being alone afterwards needs to be handled with great care.

Restorative Space

There are days when it feels
as though I am fragmented
So many pieces of myself
being given
in so many directions
and not all who demand
are careful with the pieces offered
or appreciative of the gift received
Yet to withhold
would diminish me
There are times
when I need supervision
to be restorative
and for my Supervisor
to be that person
who looks over my shoulder
as I fit the discarded shards together
especially as I discover

that not all of the pieces
slot neatly back into place
Some are now
a bit tarnished
a bit rough round the edges
and my Supervisor bears witness
as I smooth my hands over
the incomplete picture
and as I poke my fingers
where pieces are missing
Not joining me
in a frantic search
to recover the missing pieces
or to fill in the gaps
but continuing to sit with me
as I learn to love
a less than pristine picture
that shows all the signs
of wounds
and scars
gaping holes
toned down hues
that once were vibrant
and even some still shiny fragments
To sit with me
until I am remember
that all of those pieces
speak of a journey
into wholeness
a rediscovery
that I am enough.

~ Liz Crumlish

Part Three
Creative Modalities in Supervision

> 'Creative action methods 'free [supervisees] from the tunnel of words' to find colour, energy, creativity and a sense of mystery which is so often lacking in the practice of supervision.' Antony Williams [37]

The basic objective in using creative methods in supervision is to get the supervisee to show rather than to tell the issue they have brought for reflection. Due to their inherent power, creative modalities need to be treated with respect and not employed as novelties to spice things up. Novelty soon wears off whereas insight continues to yield its wisdom long after the event. The question in supervision is not 'what shall we do today for a change?' but rather 'which modality would best suit this particular supervisee to explore this particular issue?

Creative modalities come under three broad umbrellas: projection, embodiment, and role.[38]

Projective modalities

Projective modalities invite what is happening (invisibly or inaudibly) on the inside to be seen and heard on the outside. They permit

---

[37] Anthony Williams (1995) *Visual and Active supervision: Roles, Focus, Technique*, New York, London: Norton

[38] I am indebted to my friend and colleague Jane Leach for her clarity in distinguishing between projective, embodied and role modalities

'meaning and connection to emerge from the dim back-alleys of the mind to the bright lights of consciousness' main street. Finding a new, unexpected image for content that has been repetitive and imageless can help [supervisees] see and feel their situation in new ways.'[39]

Choosing objects to represent the characters or elements of a story can offer supervisees the opportunity to 'take the work from the periphery of the problem [or issue] to the core'.[40] Projective methods often bypass the clutter that comes with narration and incisively cut to the chase. The choice of an object or image can surprise supervisees as they recognise their internal dramas – their conflicts, questions, tussles - staring back at them. The experience is well summed up by Antony Williams who writes: 'visual and active supervision carries new meaning out of the dark and says "Boo!" [41]

---

[39] Williams, 161-62.
[40] Williams 162
[41] Williams, 209.

Embodied modalities

Embodied modalities take the body seriously and recognise it as a deep source of knowing and of inquiry. They can be employed to help people arrive into the supervisory space, still themselves, become aware of how they are and what is worth exploring in the session. Embodied approaches to supervision attend to body language, to bodily sensations which arise in the session and to the myriad ways in which the body speaks.

Role Modalities

Modalities which focus on role exploration are geared towards eliciting material which is largely out of the conscious awareness of supervisees. Such material may arise from within themselves (intrapersonal dynamics) or between people (interpersonal dynamics). When a supervisee names dilemmas which are characterised by 'on the one hand ... on the other hand' or 'a part of me ... but another part of me ...' then supervision through role modalities can offer a helpful way of disentangling thoughts and finding a way forward.[42]

---

[42] See Section on Role in Part Three pp 162ff.

Factors to consider

Supervisees differ enormously. Faced with a disorienting dilemma,[43] some people default to words, others to logical analysis, others again to metaphor. Some people work things out by perspiration, others by inspiration. Some doodle or draw. Others process thoughts and feelings in movement and dance. Others again in music and sound.

If supervision is to be truly hospitable, then supervisors need to ensure that the reflective modality they are proposing is a good enough 'fit' for the person to whom it is being offered. Just as there is no point asking a non-reflective person a highly reflective question, so too there is no point inviting someone who lives entirely in their head to locate the feelings that arise from the material they are presenting within their body. There are exceptions of course which can happen when people reach dead ends in their default modality. Working with a supervisee whose default approach of narration has taken them no further forward a courageous supervisor might fruitfully ask:

> Since talking doesn't seem to have got you any further forward, I wonder if you would be willing to trust me to try a completely different way of exploring this issue?'

In my experience the change in processing style from the default to the unfamiliar is often sufficient to provoke a change in understanding. When we run out

---

[43] Here I am borrowing Jack Mezirow's words to describe the kind of thing people typically bring to supervision.

of words or when words tie us up in knots rather than release us, the change in processing mode can offer a way of externalising the internal drama such that it can be seen with the eye of an observer.[44] An example:

> Jacinda is exploring why she continually says yes to unreasonable demands that are made on her. She knows she should say 'No' but continuously says yes. In supervision she talks this through and finds no change in understanding.
>
> I ask if we can try another way.
>
> 'Who have you come across in your life who knows how to say No?' I ask. 'It could be someone you know; a character in a film or in a book' [45]

Cutting across the default train of thought with left field modalities such as this can be very impactful, interrupt stuck patterns and release fresh insights.[46]

---

[44] Sometimes referred to as 'rendering the familiar strange'.
[45] This modality, the Inner Wise Guide' is spelled out in more detail later in Part Three pp 171ff.
[46] 'Supervision interrupts stuck practice and wakens us up to what we are doing. When we are awake to what we are doing we no longer sleepwalk our way through our lives.' Sheila Ryan, (2004) *Vital Practice*.

Supervision as Weaving

Our words shape the space between us.
They fall from us to be heard as they are meant.
The journey, across the abyss of separateness, is filled
with the shadows of history and talks past.
Now meaning becomes the property of the other,
to shape, to form, to turn over in the mind,
and then, to let words fall away.

Thus continues a cycle of intention, of meaning, of purpose,
blanketing time, layer on layer,
clouding the transparency of the soul.
The soul, perhaps to be delivered full and vulnerable
on the next turn, the next word.

In supervision we talk. We move one phrase upon another
to create a language of understanding and
weave a relationship of history.
The warp of our talk is the relationship.
It girds itself against the errors of our words,
the mis-spoken, the not-spoken,
the mis-understandings of our history.

The weft moves back and forth between us. You feel the
rhythm of the shaft work itself round a warp of relationship,
changing tension as it moves, creating a
pattern of woven goods that reflect the colour of our intentions and
the design of our meaning.
~ Elizabeth Holloway[47]

---

[47] Elizabeth Holloway, cited in Spy, T. (1999) 'Counselling and Psychotherapy Supervision – an ethical issue?', RACE Journal of the BACP, December 1999. Permission sought.

Objection One: 'I am just not creative'

I have often heard supervisors and supervisees say 'I am just not creative' or 'I can't draw', 'I've got two left feet'. Behind such comments there is often a misunderstanding about the role that creativity plays in the creative industries and the role creativity plays in supervision. If I commission a piece from a potter I am entitled to expect the finished product to at least meet if not exceed my expectations. But if, in supervision, I use clay to explore something that is bothering me then it is the process and not the end result that matters most: the process of choosing a lump of clay, of cutting it, shaping it, getting my hands muddy by manipulating it; perhaps the frustration of it not shaping up as I had intended, of trying again. Creativity in supervision 'is not a tool. It is a mystery that you enter: an unfolding, an opening process ... a method of self-discovery.'[48]

In my experience what matters is not whether the supervisor or supervisee are naturally gifted in the expressive arts but whether they are willing to face the supervisory quest with courage rather than timidity. Supervisors who have employed creative modalities to explore aspects of their own practice are best placed to know the power of working in such ways. First-hand experience on the part of supervisors will offer supervisees the courage and confidence they need to try new things and explore new modalities. In my experience diffidence and hesitance from supervisors in

---

[48] Natalie Rogers, (1993) *The Creative Connection: Expressive Arts as Healing*, London: PCCS

introducing new ways of working leaves supervisees insecure and weakens their containment.

Objection Two: 'I don't have time to be creative'

Some supervisors protest that they don't have time to introduce creativity into their supervision sessions. Experience proves the opposite to be true. The shorter the time available the more helpful creative approaches may be. If you want to take all day, talk about it. If you want to get to the heart of the matter quickly, focus on a word or a metaphor, an image or a movement 'Expressive arts plunge people rapidly into their inner journeys', they are not distractions.

Lia Zografou recounts how she was required to offer group supervision to large groups of staff in a very short time frame. She knew that there was no way she could supervise all twenty plus participants if she invited caseload narration. What she did was to devise a quick fire method of group supervision called the Four

Elements[49] in which supervisees succinctly name the issue they want to explore and then receive four responses: a visual response, an action response, a wisdom response and a response from experience. On average that process takes around 5 minutes per person from start to finish. Allowing for a warm up and an hospitable goodbye, ten people could be supervised in an hour through careful use of that method. When it comes to creativity in supervision, time is not the problem. Intentional focus is.

Objection Three: 'Creative modalities will do supervisors out of a job'

There is a fear among some supervisors that the use of creative modalities will do them out of a job. Interrogation of that fear often reveals a set of beliefs about supervision and the differences between uni-professional and cross-professional supervision.

Uni-professional supervision happens when two or more practitioners from the same profession meet for reflection. Supervisors who work uni-professionally inhabit the same profession as their supervisees ie a teacher supervises another teacher; a counsellor supervises another counsellor. Within that model, the supervisors' expertise lies within the domain of professional knowledge on which they draw in support of their supervisees.

---

[49] This multi-modal supervisory method is outlined in detail on page 205

By contrast, Cross-Professional Supervision happens when a supervisor meets with a practitioner from another professional discipline or line of work ie a teacher supervising a pharmacist; a youth worker supervising a nurse. Within this model, the supervisors' expertise lies in being able to facilitate reflective space and inquiry rather than on inhabiting the same field of work. When working creatively, whether uni-professionally or cross-professionally, supervisors are much more likely to be in facilitating mode, offering stage directions rather than handing out the script.

Matching Modality to Supervisory Questions

When the supervisee is struggling to find a focus for the session, projective approaches which favour distillation may help: 'I wonder if you could map this on paper/on screen?'; 'How would it be to tell this story in images using this collection of cards?' 'Could you choose things from what you have in your room to represent the key people in this situation?

When supervisees seem out of touch with the affect of the material they are exploring, projective or role approaches may help. 'Using anything in this room can you show me what it feels like to be in the place you find yourself right now?'; 'using these stones, choose three which express what is happening within you.'

A role option could be along these lines: 'I wonder if you could choose one chair to represent the person you know yourself to be and another chair to represent the person you feel you were being asked to be in the situation you are describing'.

When relationships are stuck and immutable, the use of projective modalities such as drawing the person as a building (pp 126-27) or creating visual installations representing the parties involved can externalise the internalised drama and render the familiar strange. So too a role based modality such as the Inner Wise Guide (pp 172-73) may help overcome the impasse.[50]

Hints in language

One of the best clues that a creative modality might be appropriately used arises from paying close attention to the language supervisees use in presenting their material. For example:

> Everything at work is basically ok but I've noticed each day this week that I go to work with a knot in my stomach.

On hearing 'knot in my stomach' a supervisor could choose to ignore it as a figure of speech or wonder whether it is worthy of further inquiry.

> That knot in your stomach, what size is it?
>
> How tight is that knot? ...
>
> What's the knot made of? ...

---

[50] I am indebted to my friend and colleague Jane Leach for her clarity in distinguishing between projective, embodied and role modalities in *Responsible Grace*, Methodist Church Great Britain.

How the supervisee responds to that line of exploration is highly informative

> Oh its really quite tiny … a bit like the knot you get with sewing thread …but it's so hard to unpick.
>
> Oh it is huge … about the size of my fist …
>
> It feels all jaggy and spikey as if it is made of barbed wire.

Treating the language people use in supervision, the ways they describe things, the metaphors they use, the colouring they add to their narratives etc as signs of latent meaning which have – as yet – not fully been owned by the supervisee, may be fruitful if explored with care. Caution however should be exercised in how language is presented back. Pointing out, for example, that someone has used a certain word X times in ten minutes, may leave one supervisee feeling self-conscious and guarded in what they go on to say while leaving another touched that the supervisor has been listening so intently.

The second level of seeing 'I wonder' leaves the supervisee free to say in as many words 'I don't find significance in that! End of that line of inquiry!'

With those who are open to noticing their throw away words or turns of phrase, amplifying them by slowing down the pace to focus on what has been said may prove very illuminating.

Hints in Content

Another hint that a creative modality might be profitably employed comes when the content being explored reveals some level of internal conflict. For example:

> 'An opportunity for promotion has come up at work. A part of me would love to go for it but another part of me says don't be so daft you'll never get it.'

Picking up on the parts of self which are expressed in that supervisory material the supervisor could do a number of things:

I invite you to choose a cloth to represent the part of yourself that would love to apply for that job.

(and then when the person has chosen)

I invite you to take a good look at the cloth and tell me what you notice? ….

I now invite you to stand on the cloth and speak aloud what it is about that job that you would love to go for …..

Did you notice anything about what you said or how you felt about going for the job? …

I now invite you to choose another cloth to represent that part of yourself that says 'don't be daft, you'll never get it'

(and then when the person has chosen)

> I invite you to take a good look at the cloth and tell me what you notice? ....
>
> I now invite you to stand on the cloth and speak about why you won't be applying
>
> Did you notice anything about what you said or how you felt about not going for the job? ...
>
> And now I invite you to come in the middle between the two cloths.
>
> What do you notice as you look at the part of you that says 'go for it' and the part of you that says 'don't be so daft?' ... .
>
> Where is this taking you with your question today?

When all is said and done, creative modalities are modalities: vehicles for exploring meaning and means to finding insight in the stories that supervisees bring.

Discernment

Discernment demands
that we stretch ourselves
moving beyond those places
we'd normally inhabit
with companions
we wouldn't necessarily choose.

Discernment demands
that we become vulnerable
open to scrutiny
conjecture
and even brutality

Discernment demands
that we place ourselves
in the glare of the spotlight
where others will judge

the light and the shade.
Discernment demands
that we hope and imagine ourselves
into a new way of being
that may never come to fruition.

Discernment demands
that we submit wholly
to the will of God
taking the first steps
on a journey
destination unknown.

That journey of discernment
is one not taken lightly
but with courage and integrity
with the only certainty
that all will be changed
All except - that we remain
Beloved of God.

~ Liz Crumlish

Let the creativity do the talking

Word based supervision typically takes the form of a conversation between the supervisor and the supervisee about some aspect of the supervisee's soul as it finds expression in their role and context. The character of such conversation is interpersonal. Creative modalities, however, invite supervisees to primarily converse with themselves. In such cases, the role of the supervisor is as facilitator of an internalised conversation which becomes externalised in sound, or image, or fabric or movement etc. Once a supervisee is engaged in exploring their issue through use of a creative modality, that modality should be invited to do the talking. Examples:

> What does that knot have to say to you?
>
> What do you want to say to it? Try it!
>
> How would it be to untie it?
>
> How would it be to refuse to take it to work tomorrow?

One of the temptations that supervisors with little experience in working creatively are prone to is to conduct the supervisory session as if the image, or movement or metaphor had never been introduced. I have seen supervisees find significant resonance with an object they have chosen only to have a supervisor silence the voice of that object by inviting the supervisee to have a conversation with them (the supervisor) about it. Letting the object, the image, the movement or the metaphor do the talking is the best policy every time.

Lastly, I would urge supervisors not to interpret what happens. Notice the difference between

> 'I wonder what has happened to that knot in the last five minutes while you have been smiling.'

And

> 'You are clearly smiling because that knot has gone.'

The former underlines the truth that the authority on the supervisee is the supervisee. The latter smacks of 'supervisor knows best' in claiming the authority to interpret the supervisee.

I would also caution supervisors against interpreting and even naming the objects or images the supervisee chooses.

> 'I see you have placed four buttons on the table'

> 'Those are not buttons, those are my four colleagues'

Much better to ask' 'so what have we here?' than to presume that buttons are buttons, toy guns are weapons, bricks mean the supervisee wants to build something. Asking 'what story are you telling by the items you have chosen?' leaves the supervisee much more room for playful adventure. After all, the supervisee's need to explore should always trump the supervisor's need to understand. Facilitating exploration is the name of the game not information exchange. Supervisors who stay out of the way leave more room for the supervisee to make the space their own.

Assembling your own creative kit

Specialist pre-made creative kits are available for purchase but nothing beats creating your own over time. At the risk of being over prescriptive here are some items which might usefully be included in a small world kit. Some of them can be sourced in the children's section of larger supermarkets, Charity shops are another good source. Items that would otherwise be discarded such as spent batteries or light bulbs which have blown are also very handy to hang on to. For fabrics anything between the straw handles on a paper shopping bag through gift ribbons to metre lengths of assorted cloths can all be included. The sky is the limit. Let your inner hunter-gatherer out and enjoy rummaging through forgotten drawers.

Making your own Small World Kit

Human figurines (male, female, adult, child)

Animals (domestic, wild, land, sea, air)

Finger puppets

Soft and cuddly items. Hard edged items

Stones and shells of varying weights, sizes, colours, textures

Buttons (range of colours, materials, uses)

Things which suggest ways forward (compass, arrows, signposts, old keys)

Things which suggest boundaries (gates, doors, fences, road blocks, luggage padlocks)

Shiny things , Dark things

Symbols of communication (phone, post box etc)

Symbols of violence (plastic guns, handcuffs, knife)

Symbols of fun (miniature drink bottle, party poppers, champagne cork)

Symbols of insight (glasses or lenses from broken glasses)

Broken objects are good to include as long as they are not dangerous to touch (eg a pair of glasses with a lens missing; piece of a broken plant pot)

Ribbons of different colours, textures, lengths and sizes

Things people associate with joy and of sadness

Things pertaining to energy (batteries, light bulbs. fuses)

Things which can be assembled for construction (lego pieces; screws; nuts, bolts)

Thread, string, scrunched up wire from spiral bound notebooks

Toy vehicles and modes of transport

Bouncy ball …..

Do not overlook the ordinary

Although having a special kit or small world collection may have its advantages given the extensive range it offers, every space in which supervision is conducted has ordinary 'stuff' which can be utilised: chairs, curtains, rugs, pictures on walls, coffee cups, pens, rubber bands, staplers, waste paper basket, electric sockets, light switches, tissues etc. Don't forget whatever the supervisee has on their person: the clothes they are wearing; a piece of jewellery; the coins in their purse; the things in their handbag or rucksack; their shoe laces; belts; glasses; wedding rings ... There is no limit to what can be gainfully employed when working creatively.

Whatever you collect and however you choose to conduct supervision let the words of Noel Davis be an encouragement to you as you creatively engage.

> Venture beyond the familiar
> Range wider than routine
> Delve beneath the certain
> Hold truth with an open heart.
> Break from the programmed whatever it be.
> Take a different way home.[51]

---

[51] Noel Davis (2011) *Together at the Edge: Trust Me*, Narooma, NSW: Lifeflow Education. Used with permission of the author.

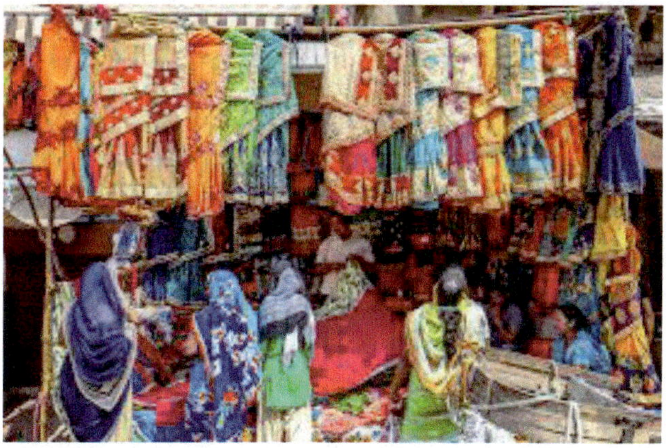

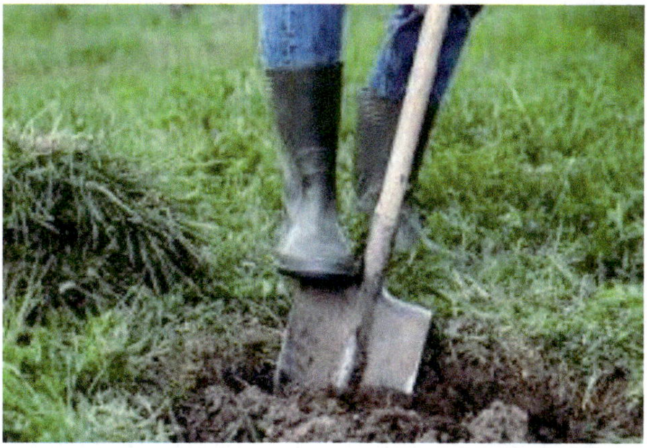

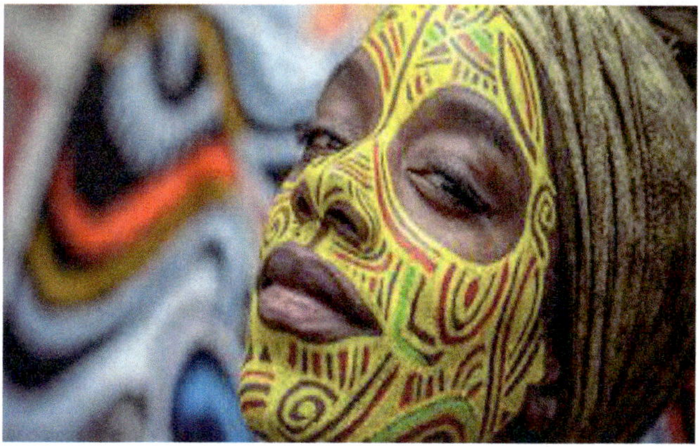

Part Four
Creative Supervision
in Practice

Imagery & Art

> Art is a direct visceral experience. It does not need to go through the word mill. Colour, line and form can reveal our energy levels, our feeling states and our self-concepts. Colour can be soft or intense, brilliant or dull, delicate or powerful. Line can be jagged or smooth, flowing or disconnected, simple or complicated. All bear kinaesthetic messages.'[52]

As a form of projective supervision there is no end to what you can do with visual images. These could be an assortment of postcards which you have personally gathered or a ready-made collection which is available for purchase.[53] The key to any collection of images is to ensure breadth and range. Ideally an image collection will have a mixture of dark and light, bright and gloomy. It will also want to combine things which are generally regarded as attractive or appealing with images of things which are less so. In supervision, participants need to be able to recognize themselves and see their experiences mirrored back to them in the images available. Having a range of cards allows people to find validation for the breadth of experiences they encounter, the multiple layers of identities that work brings out in them and the range of responses that professional life evokes. In my experience, the dialogue between soul, role and context can often be easier to see than to hear.

---

[52] Natalie Rogers, (1993) *Creative Connection*, 69.
[53] Examples include Evoke cards www.evoke.com; Envision Cards used by the NHS in Scotland. See p 133

> **Using imagery to help supervisees arrive**
>
> Choose an image which represents you as a person arriving here today.
>
> Choose a second image which represents what your role requires of you today.
>
> Looking at the images you have chosen
>
> What do you see or notice?
>
> What causes you to wonder or turn things over in your mind?
>
> What connections do you make?
>
> What do you realize?
>
> What are the implications for your work role?

Using imagery to find a supervisory focus

'Images have a way of bypassing the chatter of our logical minds and nudging our deep soul wisdom where intuitive answers can be found and spoken.'[54] When someone is not clear what to focus on in supervision you could ask them to choose a few cards which somehow speak to their experience at work since you last met together. Once they have chosen, you could ask which of these cards interests them the most and then invite them to tell the story behind the card choice.

---

[54] Seena Frost, (2010). *SoulCollage® Evolving: An Intuitive Collage Process for Self-Discovery and Community*. Santa Cruz: Hanford Mead Publishers.

Once again, remember to let the images do the talking. Don't abandon the image prematurely in favour of talking *about* the issue as if the image was not itself a valuable voice in the conversation. Go back again and again to the image. Use the notice, wonder, realize model. Name the obvious.

Three levels of Seeing in Practice

'I notice that you are focusing on the jagged edges which protrude from each of the wooden spokes. But I see that some of them are actually rounded.'

'I notice you are talking about how each of those wooden posts plays it part in creating a circle but I notice they don't do that in a uniform way.'

'I realise from where I am sitting that I cannot find a way to access the circle of green grass at the centre of the image and wonder where you see the entry points?'

Creating Visual Images

An alternative to choosing pre-made images is to have some art materials and paper available for supervisees to make their own images. A simple kit might include pencils, erasers, sharpener, ruler, felt pens, pastels and coloured crayons. Supervisees could then be offered five minutes to make an image which expresses something of how work has been for them in recent times. Once the five minutes is up they could be invited to say what they see or notice as they look, what makes them curious or causes them to wonder and what they realise as they look at the image they have created.

Visual art is not the prerogative of the artist or the painter. Stick figures quickly drawn with a ballpoint pen on a scrap piece of paper may be highly illuminating for someone trying to get a handle on dynamics at work. In supervision, the visual image is made in pursuit of insight. It is the exploratory process that matters more than the finished product.

Without specialist knowledge, skills or training, a courageous supervisor might invite supervisees to draw the issue they are bringing to supervision in whatever way they like. Then using that image the supervisor might ask

> What do you notice as you look at your drawing?

Very often when people draw the issue they want to bring to supervision they leave themselves out of it. If the supervisor gets a sense that this might be the case she might ask:

'And are you here?'

That question often comes as a surprise to supervisees and becomes a catalyst for further inquiry.

'I wonder if you want to be here (ie in the picture)?'

'I wonder where you would place yourself?'

Offering what the supervisor notices back to the supervisee continues the exploration

'I notice you have placed yourself at some distance from the other stick figures.'

'I notice you have placed yourself off the page.'

Noticing without interpreting, wondering without directing needs practice.

Gregg Furth[55] offers supervisors some pointers to use in response to the images that supervisees make.

---

[55] Gregg M Furth (1988) *The Secret World of Drawings: A Jungian Approach to Healing through Art*, Inner City Books.

Focal Points to Explore Drawings

What **Feeling** does the image convey. This can be illuminating in eliciting the atmosphere before going into the seeing and noticing of the elements.

What is **Central**? Does it indicate the core of the issue or what is important to the supervisee. Look at top, bottom, left and right, foreground (what is nearest) and background (what is in the distance).

Size. Notice the proportions. Is something being emphasised or minimised?

Perspective. Notice the perspective from which the image is seen. Is it ground up or an aerial view. What arouses your curiosity? Where is the supervisee or where would they like to be in relation to the issue?

Edging. Notice what is at the edge of the frame, crossing the boundary of the frame or partially shown. Wonder aloud what this could mean.

Barriers. Notice any barriers, figures or objects which block other parts of the image from being seen. Are these significant?

What is missing? Wonder aloud what could be absent or left out of the image. How does what is absent or omitted relate to the supervisees life and work?

Guided drawing

Another way of creating visual imagery in supervision is through guided drawing. Here is an example which could be used in individual or group supervision.

Guided Drawing Exercise

Make sure people have plenty of personal space.
Give each person a sheet of paper and a choice of coloured pens or crayons.
Invite a moment to quiet to settle down
Hosting & Containing

Think of someone you work with whom you would like a better relationship.
'What is it about that person or that relationship that bothers or concerns you?
Eliciting and Focusing
Now take an imaginative leap and imagine that person as a building – and briefly sketch that out on paper using the coloured pens.
Exploring & Imagining
To indicate you have finished please put down your pens. ...
Now on that sheet of paper place yourself in relation to that building.
Exploring & Imagining
and again to indicate you have finished put down your pens.

Invite people to come and sit together in clusters.

What you are asked to do is to present the artistic representation of the person you have been thinking about and the relationship you have with them to the rest of the group without using any words whatsoever.

What those who receive your presentation will offer you back is what they see, notice and wonder. Presenters are asked not to explain or to respond.
Exploring & Imagining

After everyone has presented and received feedback, ask people to go back to their private space and in the light of the feedback they received make one adjustment to their drawing that represents a way of taking that relationship forward.
Bridging & Enacting

Once again when finished put pens down, invite participants to regroup.
Once again invite people to present their artwork to their peers without words.
Invite peers to say what they see or notice.

Once everyone has feedback, invite each person in turn to say as succinctly as possible what insight they have gained by reflecting in this way.
Reviewing & Closing

But I can't draw

Paul Klee famously said that to draw is to 'take a line for a walk' and that 'a line is a dot going for a walk'. Those who are hesitant to draw might like to think of it as simply making a mark. Meeting hesitance with playfulness can help as can limiting the time involved using for example an egg timer or an on screen digital countdown. Mark making in supervision can take many forms: doodles, sketches, scribbles, cut and paste collage, clay or plasticine modelling etc. Online forms of drawing include zoom whiteboard, Miro and Stop Motion.

Photography

Photography offers a natural form of contemplative exploration due to its inherent invitation to look, look and look again at something that catches the eye. With cameras on smart phones, photography can easily be used as an exploratory modality in supervision. Supervisees could be asked to bring a photo diary of their month from which they might select two or three work situations to explore in further depth. Or, at the beginning of a session, supervisees could be invited to leave the supervisory space to take photographs of anything (indoors or outdoors) which somehow speaks to their experience at work. Once back in the supervisory space they could use the photographs in a number of ways: they could simple talk about them; they could reverse roles with the photographs and give them voice; they could create dialogues between photographs; they could journal under headings such as 'you speak to me of...' 'you challenge me to ...'

The purpose of photography in supervision – as with all creative modalities – is to render the familiar strange ie to enable the supervisee to see themselves, their role and their contexts through different eyes and to gain fresh perspectives. As such, photographs become 'icons of a new awareness. Through iconization (projecting and associating meaning into photographs) we arrive at meaningful words (a new narrative) to denote what we bodily feel or sense.'[56]

Working with textiles

The kinaesthetic nature of knitting, felting, crafting and working with wool and fabric in which textures are continuously handled offer a contemplative way of exploring a supervisory issue. Liz Crumlish writes:

'For over a year now, since the first pandemic stay at home measure in the UK, I have been crocheting hearts.

I now have hundreds of crocheted hearts. Made from all sorts of yarn, they are of different shapes and sizes, colours and textures. There has been solace in carefully crafting each, a rhythm that has provided comfort and balm.

I am not yet clear what I will do with them and so they are left unfinished, no ends neatly sewn in or and tidied away.

---

[56] For more on this see Sitvast J. (2021). *How Nurses can Facilitate Meaning-making and Dialogue: Reflections on Narrative and Photo Stories.* Cambridge Scholars Publishing.

Those untidy tails of yarn may be needed in the fashioning of something bigger.

These hearts seem to capture something of the tentativeness of the world as some areas emerge from pandemic and as others remain locked in the grip of trauma with no end in sight. Unfinished, it seems, is the shape of things to come.

Perhaps we know how to be when one thing ends and the next is already in sight, perhaps even within our grasp. But how might we meet those we supervise in those unfinished spaces and how might we be with them in what may be a prolonged phase of transition? How will we continue to engage in the restorative and transformative work of supervision? Re-membering and re-storying will be important elements of recovery and emergence from global trauma.'

Supervision and Weaving

The contraflow nature of weaving, in which the warp provides the scaffolding for the story and the weft the emerging pattern, provides a very effective way of seeing a supervisory issue in 3D. Balancing warp and weft takes skill as does the choice of materials not all of which work well together. Tears, holes, snaps, uneven tension all provide opportunities for recognition in supervision. A simple form of weaving can also be done with paper and paint.

Weaving with Paper

On a large sheet of paper and using whatever colours you have to hand, depict the highpoint of your working life in recent weeks.

On another sheet of paper, depict the low point of your working life in recent weeks.

Tear each picture into strips of equal width and weave them together.

What do you see?

What cause you to wonder?

What do you realise?

Soul Collage®

SoulCollage® is a gentle, playful and often joyful way of exploring. Using images from magazines, individuals create their own unique deck of cards, where each card represents a different aspect of themselves. The process combines image, words, intuition, and synchronicity into a unique creative and artistic process that anyone can do. It requires no special skills, but can often produce images and insights that are surprising and full of depth and meaning. SoulCollage® works directly with the language of symbols, images and archetypes and is an insightful process of self-discovery. For those who want to buy ready-made cards Seena Frost has produced four sets of images: *Committee Suit* is made up of images representing the different voices that constitute our personalities. The *Community Suit* cards represent the things that influence us ie friends, family, pets, historical figures, special places etc. The *Companions Suit* relates to chakras. The *Council Suit* consists of Jungian archetypes important in our life journeys.[57]

Other Creative Media

There are far more ways of incorporating visual imagery in supervision than I have identified here. Knitting, working with plasticine, playdoh or clay all offer rich seams of exploration. Furthermore the kinaesthetic nature that is inherent in making and crafting adds committed effort and investment to the exploratory process.

There is a growing range of computer based software and apps for drawing and comic creation including: Photoshop CC; Clip Studio Paint; Paint Tool SAI ; Paintstorm Studio; MediBang Paint Pro; Corel Painter 2021; Krita and GIMP2; Stop motion.

---

[57] Seena Frost (2010) *SoulCollage® Evolving: An Intuitive Collage Process for Self-Discovery and Community*. Santa Cruz: Hanford Mead Publishers

Ready Made Image Collections

Sets of cards which are readily available include Evoke cards from evoke.com; Emotions Cards by Tiffany Watt Smith and Therese Vandling; MetaFox Pack of 52 Motivational Postcards for Coaching and Therapy; Signposts from Innovativeresources.org. Catherine Anderson has produced books of imagery entitled *The Creative Photographer, Journaling the Labyrinth Path* and *Collage Imagery*. www.creativepilgrimage.com

To follow up

Monica Carpendale (2011) *A Traveller's Guide to Art Therapy Supervision,* Victoria, Canada: Trafford Publishing

Barbara Fish, (2016) *Art-Based Supervision: Cultivating Therapeutic Insight Through Imagery,* London: Routledge

Liesl Silverstone, (2009) *Art Therapy Exercises: Inspirational and Practical Ideas to Stimulate the Imagination*, London: Jessica Kingsley

Showing up

Into this room you
bring me you,
all that is seen and unseen.
This space is yours
for what you need
to bring and do.

I come into this room too
but step aside from me
offering only the calm
of this moment and place.

You speak, I hear.
I see, I wonder.
I feel your unspoken anxiety
and know not where my own
has appeared from.

My hands are agitated
just like your feet and ankles
I feel my pulse anything but calm
and wonder what is unseen
and unspoken by you
in your words and the picture
you brought into this room.

Let me see and wonder
some more.

I invite you to work
with the picture you
brought into this room

somewhere in there is
something waiting to burst into life
or something waiting to be let go.

As you look and wonder
awaiting the realisation
to set you free from
the anxiety
we both experienced
know that you
bring all the
gifts into this space
to find the kernel of
life and lifegiving work.

This kernel, this seed
is not anxious but awaits
the right conditions
which you have sown
and tended and ready
for another harvest.

~ Sarah Murray

Sound & Music

The artist's hand 'causes vibrations in the soul'.
Vassily Kandinsky pianist and painter

Simone Weil tells a story about two prisoners in adjoining cells who learn, over a very long period of time, to talk to each other by tapping on the wall. 'The wall is the thing which separates them, but it is also their means of communication,' she writes. 'Every separation is a link.'[58] We could say that Supervision

> 'is about that wall. It's about our desire to talk, to understand and be understood. It's also about listening to each other, not just the words but the gaps in between. ... It isn't a magical process. It's something that is a part of our everyday lives – we tap, we listen.'[59]

In supervision we open our ears and hearts to deeper levels of listening through which we hear not only the stories that supervisees bring, but also the myriad of ways they express them through variations in tone, pitch, rhythm, and pulse. Once we tap into the sonic experience of our supervisees, we then have the opportunity to reflect back through the medium of sound through which we can engage supervisees in a deeper form of dialogue. This kind of deep listening and reflection does not require musical skills, talent, or experience; it is accessible to all of us if we are willing to

---

[58] Cited in Stephen Grosz (2013) *The Examined Life: How We Lose and Find Ourselves,* London: Chatto & Windus
[59] Grosz (2013) *The Examined Life*

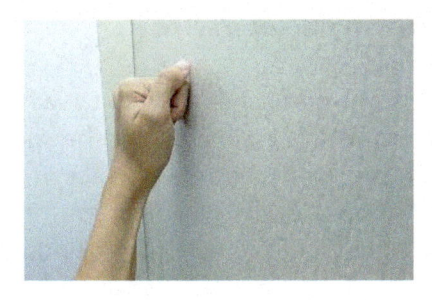

explore our own innate responsiveness to sound. Sonic modalities in supervision range from tapping on walls to humming, rhythmic clapping to beating a drum, instrumental improvisation, experimenting with voice, pitch and tone to full blown musical compositions with everything in between.

Voice links breath, body, soul and emotion in a primitive, pre-verbal and pre-cognitive way. The mind only joins in later. 'Our vocal chords, located between our head and body, are the channel through which we link these aspects of self.'[60] But just as many people have internalised a script which says 'I am not creative' or 'I cannot draw' so too, many have been told 'you are too loud' or 'speak up I can't hear you'. And if that is so of the spoken word it is even more so of singing. Giving supervisees 'permission' for their sound to be 'good enough' may reconnect them with their innate musicality and rhythm: the rhythm of the heartbeat, the rhythm of walking, the rhythm of the seasons.

As children we spontaneously sing, blissfully unaware of the sounds we are making. As we grow up, in response to the message we receive, we learn to 'tone it down' or to save our singing for the shower or the football terraces. Sadly too many voices go unheard muffled by a blanket of self-consciousness and imminent shame. 'Whenever you stopped singing' says Angie Arrien, 'is when you lost your soul.' Supervisors who enable supervisees to connect with their own vibrations are engaged in 'soul retrieval work'.[61]

---

[60] Natalie Rogers (1993) *Creative Connection*, 81
[61] Angie Arrien cited in Rogers (1993)

Using sound before meeting a supervisee

Gathering ourselves, in body, mind and spirit into whole beings is a form of self-care which enables us to be more hospitable to others. Given the primal nature of voice, it can be helpful to prepare for vocalisation by paying attention to our own rhythmic breathing and allowing it to ground and stabilise us. (See suggestions in the Embodiment and Movement section 148ff.) Once grounded and aware of our own unique rhythmic pulse, a vocalisation exercise such as the following can heighten our awareness.

Vocalisation

Close your eyes, open your mouth and allow yourself to play around with your sound, up and down, until you find a vibration that you are comfortable with.

Try and find a sound that comes from deep down in your belly. Feel it jiggle inside you warming your gullet. Be playful and let it jump around as you laugh or chuckle or grunt or sigh.

Allow breathing space between sounds. Simply open your mouth and let go. Whatever sound you make let it come from your belly.

Become aware of the sounds you are drawn to and those which surprise you. Become aware also to the tone or pitch you use. Are the sounds monotone or lyrical? Is the pitch drawn from a narrow or a wider range.[62]

---

[62] Adapted from 'Finding your own Note' cf Rogers (1993) 38-39.

Sound in hosting

As part of the hosting process at the beginning of the session, supervisors could guide supervisees through the exercise above or help them explore vibration based on each of the vowels as follows.

> Placing one hand on your chest feel the different vibrations which arise from elongating the sounds. A...E...I...O...U... The combination of making the sounds and feeling the vibrations will help supervisees release, relax and lower tension.[63]

Recorded music could also be used to ease supervisees transitions into the supervisory space giving them time to settle and become present.[64] Having one or two short reflective pieces on your phone or desktop means they are accessible when needed and can be used equally effectively whether meeting in person or on a digital platform. Perhaps your supervisee has music of their own which they could use to help them arrive into the space.

---

[63] Cf Don Campbell (1989) *The Roar of Silence*, Wheaton, IL: Theosophical Publishing House.
[64] Try for example *Spiegel im Spiegel* by Arvo Pärt or *Sketches of Light* by Scottish composer Alexander Chapman Campbell.

Sound in Eliciting and Focusing

Since music is so evocative and causes vibrations in the soul, supervisors could attend to eliciting and focusing by a range of invitations

> 'If you think about your work at the moment, is there a song that comes to mind or a piece of music that sums it up for you?'

With a random range of materials available in the room, a supervisor could say

> 'Using anything you find, could you let me hear how it is for you at work?'

Or in response to a comment like 'my head is so full of noise' the supervisor could say:

> 'If you were to let that noise out what sound would it make?'

Supervisees do not need any musical training to play random notes on a piano or thump loudly on a bass drum. In response to the sounds expressed, supervisors could use the three levels of seeing to ask what supervisees noticed, wondered or realised from the sounds they made or the process of making them. 'I noticed my hesitancy. I wanted to really crash the cymbal but ending up lightly touching it'. Staying in the role of witness, the supervisor might then say what they noticed as they listened. 'I felt a sense of disconnection between the irritation you named in telling your story and the gentleness of the sound you expressed. I wonder if that resonates with you?'

Sound in Exploring

One of my most memorable experiences of using sound as an exploratory medium in supervision was in a group session led by a music therapist who, instead of bringing along a range of exotic musical instruments which only a specialist would have, laid down in the middle of the floor a range of plastic and paper bags, pens, an assortment of drinking mugs and glasses, pencils, elastic bands, half blown and fully blown balloons. As a group we were invited to discover what sounds we could make by tapping the glasses with a pencil, crunching up the paper bags, rustling the plastic ones, pinging the elastic bands and squeezing air out of the balloons. We were also encouraged to experiment with our bodies 'as instruments' by tapping or clapping, snapping our fingers etc. Once the group had overcome its self-consciousness we were then invited one by one to reflect on how work had been for each of us in recent weeks and then to find a sound or series of sounds to express its impact upon us. To my surprise I found myself blowing raspberries into the comb from my back pocket. The noise was ugly and distasteful. But the resonance was deep. In thirty seconds I had accessed and expressed what had been rumbling around inside me but had, until then, been unable to confront. Using a modality which enabled me to 'hear the inside, out' was cathartic and helped me to find what I needed to dislodge a stuck dynamic at work.

Music making in exploring

One of the great advantages of supervising online, is that supervisees are often in their own home settings surrounded by their own things. In one such session I could see a guitar in the corner of the screen. I tentatively asked if the supervisee would be willing to incorporate music into our session. 'It's out of tune' she said 'and needs restrung'. The metaphor did not escape me. I said nothing. 'A bit like me I suppose' she said and with that picked up the guitar and began to tune it. 'Are we still talking about the guitar or about yourself I asked?'

When working with supervisees who play musical instruments I sometimes invoke music and sound as our conversational modality. 'Can you let me hear how the last month has been for you at work?' I ask. Two experiences of doing this in supervision stand out over the years.

The first was with an accomplished pianist who thought for a moment and then picked out the melody line of 'three blind mice' with one finger. When he had finished I asked him 'What did you notice?' His response brought him to tears. 'It was all staccato with no accompaniment'. 'Is that how work has been for you these last few weeks?' I asked. 'Absolutely' came the reply. And with a genuine and heartfelt offer to accompany him the session took off.

The second memorable experience was with a supervisee who ran out of words. 'I've been doing everything I can to be accommodating at work' she said 'but its doing my head in and I can't figure out what to do next.' 'I know you play the piano' I said 'and wonder if we could continue the session from there?' Once relocated at the piano I asked her to make an authentic sound using the keyboard.

Without hesitation she produced a range of loud crashing chords. I then asked her what 'trying to be accommodating at work' sounded like. She spontaneously played a series of harmonic arpeggios which seemed to flow easily. I invited her to say what she had noticed from what she had played. 'I only let the harmony out at work' she said 'the crashing chords come out at home'.

Using Sound in exploring Soul, Role and Context

Music which has a definite musical pattern can effectively be used to help supervisees reflect on the deep patterns within their life and practice. Such music works best when chosen by supervisees themselves since this is more likely to have meaning for them. With groups I have used *Canon in D* by Johann Pachelbel to explore the 'canon' (or repetitive structure) of someone's work and what might be termed the 'variations'.

In exploring soul, I have also found *Mazuzu's Dream* by Max Richter very effective. *Mazuzu's Dream* is a composition for six pianos which opens with a bass line comprising five notes which sustains the piece throughout its nine minute duration. As each of the other five pianos is added, the music is at times jazzy and playful, at other times frenzied and chaotic. Only the beat and the bass line remain constant. I have used the piece to help supervisees to explore the bass line in their own lives (their soul) which at times may be hard to hear in their role (the demanding melodies they play at work) and the sheer noise of those work contexts. It is striking just how many people lose the bass line after a few bars and only hear the din of the music which surrounds it.[65] I devised this exercise in response to this invitation by Dietrich Bonhoeffer:

> 'Pin your faith in the cantus firmus [because] where the ground bass is firm and clear, there is nothing to stop the counterpoint from being developed to the utmost of its limits without confusion or collapse.'[66]

Bonhoeffer's cantus firmus – his bass line – was what got him through imprisonment and torture by the Nazis. In the context of such degradation and dehumanisation his words speak powerfully to practitioners struggling to hang on to their soul within the competing demands of their role and context. Writing from his own convictions he speaks of his need to

> 'hang on to my cantus firmus, that deep rhythmic sustaining pulse which undergirds me; that melody which plays within me; that tune to which my two left feet dance.'

Supervisors know how hard it can be to hang on to our 'cantus firmus', that deep rhythmic pulse which undergirds us, that melody which plays within us; that tune to which our two left feet dance. And yet practice without it becomes soulless and work burdensome. Burnout begins when we

---

[65] I am indebted to Debbie Ford for introducing me to Mazuzu's Dream at a supervision workshop I ran in Cambridge ten years ago. An extract may be heard here https://soundcloud.com/pianocircus/max-richter-mazuzu-dream

[66] Dietrich Bonhoeffer was a German pastor who was incarcerated by the Nazis for standing up against Hitler. He wrote this from his prison cell in 1944 shortly before his execution.

lose touch with our why. Thankfully, soulful supervision offers a way back from the brink.

Assembling a Sound Collection

Assemble your own sound kit using a range of musical and percussive items. Ordinary things like plastic and paper bags which rustle; pens or sticks which can be used as beaters; mugs and glasses which respond differently to the tap of a pencil; elastic bands or things which ping when stretched; half blown and fully blown balloons which squeal when blown and squelch when released; whistles and bells; keys which jangle; drums; kazoos; mouth organs etc

To follow up

Campbell, D. (1989) *The Roar of Silence*, Wheaton, IL: Theosophical Publishing House.

Odell-Miller, H. and Richards, E. (2007) *Supervision of Music Therapy: A Theoretical and Practical Handbook,* London: Routledge

Richardson, H. (2009), 'A Musical Metaphor for Pastoral Supervision', *Practical Theology* 2 (3): 373-86.

All tuned up and ready to go
each takes their place
and there is a hush
a moment suspended
that is filled with expectancy
until the baton falls
and the silence is broken
sometimes tentatively
by a gentle melody
sometimes violently
by a crashing cacophony
The lead changes hands
moving seamlessly
from one to the other
Deep resonant bass notes
High haunting grace notes
Rhythmic percussion
combining to share a story
not always finding
resolution
but, together
working toward completion
And then, task accomplished
each sustained
by having played a part
there is renewed energy
as each returns to solo practice.

~ Liz Crumlish

Embodiment & Movement

The body is the most communicative organ we have. We touch, we shake hands, we hug, we kiss, we embrace. We clench, we release, we grip, we let go, we crash around, we move mindfully, we caress, we make love. We are not no-body. We are some-body. 'Before anything else, we are feeling bodies.'[67] As Barbara Mettler writes:

> 'Movement is our primary medium of expression, upon which all other means depend. Speaking, writing, singing, drawing, painting, using any tool or instrument, building, all begin with a movement impulse which is then transformed into word, tone, line, colour or some other material. In every other medium our inner experience is externalised in some material apart from ourselves. In movement .. our own body is the material. Material and instrument and idea are one in the expressively moving body.'[68]

Since our bodies are givens, why would they not play a part in supervision? Why would we send all our exploration *upwards* to the head and not *downwards* into our naturally playful bodies? An embodied approach to supervision begins with supervisors being at home in their own skin. Grounding ourselves before supervisees arrive, enhances our capacity for effective and intentional presence. Tuning into the body allows supervisors to 'hear from the *me* that

---

[67] John Cromby (2015) *Feeling Bodies: Embodying Psychology*, Basingstoke: Palgrave Macmillan, 1
[68] Barbara Mettler 'The art of Body Movement' in Rogers, (1993) 50.

I don't know so well'.[69] Some examples that supervisors could use:

Softening the Jaw

Stand or sit with your feet shoulder width apart, relax your forehead, soften your jaw, drop your shoulders and allow your arms to go limp by your side. Slow your breathing down, breath out the tensions and settle into a comfortable rhythm breathing for 2-3 minutes allowing tension to drain away.

Body Shake

Rotate your shoulders and arms back and forward, give your arms a shake - one way then the other - to release the muscle tension. Then, stand up straight, open up your rib cage by stretching your shoulders back and drop your arms by your side. Take a few slow deep breaths in and out and allow your breathing to fall back into a slower more relaxed pace.

---

[69] E. T. Gendlin in Koch et al. (2012) *Body Memory, Metaphor and Movement*, Amsterdam: John Benjamin Publishing, 79.

Breathing Exercise (Seated)

Sit on a chair with your feet on the ground. Eyes closed or focused on a spot.

1. Acknowledging
Bring yourself into the present moment by connecting with the floor beneath and the chair supporting you. Ask 'what is going on for me right now?' Acknowledge sensations, thoughts and feelings. Notice how you move or shift but without analysis or judgment.

2. Gathering
Become aware of your breathing ... in .. and out ... in ... and out.
In heightening your awareness of your breath do not try and change it.
Allow your breath to anchor you in the present moment.

3. Expanding
Expand your awareness from your breath to the whole of your body.
Become aware of your body in time.
Become aware of your skin, your outer boundary.
Now expand your awareness to the space in front of you, behind you, to your left and to your right.
Become aware of the space below you and the space above you.[70]

---

[70] Adapted from Olga Levitt in Bownas and Fredman (2017), *Working with Embodiment in Supervision*, London: Routledge 136

Body Scan (Standing)

Standing up, feet slightly apart, hands loosely by your sides, feel the floor beneath your feet. Let your weight sink into the floor knowing that it can support you.

Allow your consciousness to travel from your feet through your ankles to your knees.
Allow your knees to bend and feel the spring they allow you.

Allow yourself to become conscious of your tummy.
Breathe into it noticing how it is today.
Is it tense or relaxed? Is it knotted or fluid?
Breathe into that space.

Allow your attention to come into your chest
Noticing your breathing …in and out … in and out.
Let your breathing support you as you wriggle your shoulders releasing any cricks and tensions, feeling them rest and rise

Take your attention up through your neck and feel the weight of your head.

Allow your head to roll from side to side.

And rest … grounded … fluid and ready for the supervisee who is about to arrive.

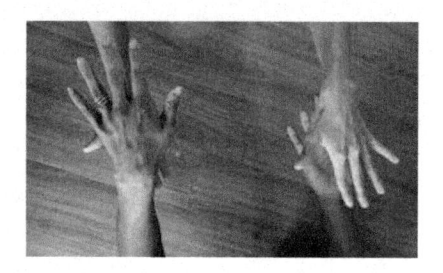

Embodied beginnings

Having grounded ourselves, we are now ready to open the door to our supervisees or admit them online. A variation on this approach can be used as part of the hosting process at the beginning of a group supervision session. If done online then screenshare can be used. Invite participants to find a space in the room which allows them room to respond to the words with their own actions if they wish.

Embodied Exercise for Beginning

Reaching downwards and delving,
we are rooted in our true ground.
Reaching upwards and yearning,
we look to all which lies beyond.
Opening our arms wide to welcome our neighbour,
we embrace the stranger as a friend.
Reaching backwards into the past,
we absorb what is good and are thankful.
Reaching forwards into the future,
we give of ourselves in trust.
Being still in the present,
we rest in the silence of being.[71]

---

[71] I have been unable to trace the origin of this text.

Embodiment in co-creating the space

Another way of helping people to arrive into the space is to invite them to walk around the perimeter of the room; to feel the walls that will hold them; to stand at the lintel of the door by which they came in and by which they will go out; to sense the space the room provides. In supervising a group, the co-creation of the space can be amplified by inviting people to decorate the room in any way they wish: by draping the walls with cloths; indicating the boundary of the space with ribbons, cords or rope etc.

Embodied supervision outdoors

I have engaged in supervision on the beach, on a mountain trail, in a city street surrounded by sandstone tenements, in a park, on a canal walkway, each of which fed and nurtured the reflective process. There is something about the physicality of moving outdoors, with a micro-contract in place to ensure that the space is safe, intentional and boundaried that can enhance rather than dilute reflexive inquiry.

Engaging with outdoor space, with sound, with symbol, with story, with ritual and the sheer effort of putting one foot in front of the other, can help to get beneath the words to the core of the supervisory question. With body and not only mind engaged, emotions are likely to be unearthed and dormant feelings awakened.

Embodiment in Eliciting & Focusing

The body can inform supervisees know what it is that they want to explore in supervision. Inviting someone to express their feelings through the body offers a form of 'moving from the inside, out'. Whether the movements are graceful or grotesque, inviting or repelling, the body does not lie. When a supervisee does not know what they are feeling, inviting them to close their eyes and allow their body to start moving becomes a form of self-discovery. If the supervisee feels self-conscious then the supervisor can either offer to close their eyes and not watch, or, in the case of working online, invite the supervisee to switch off their camera while moving.

As part of the eliciting process, supervisees could be asked to let the past month or so of work to pass before their eyes and to move freely. After 'moving from the inside out' they could be asked what they noticed as they moved. After they have spoken, the supervisor might speak as a witness – not an observer, nor as an interpreter – but as a witness. Witness responses share the impact the movement had on the supervisor. 'When you fell to your knees, I felt a sense of letting go', 'when you started running around the room I felt unable to keep up with your pace'. The purpose of any witness response from the supervisor is not to engage the supervisee in conversation with the supervisor but rather to facilitate and deepen the supervisee's inner process. Within every witness response lies the question: 'Does what I have witnessed have any resonance for you?'

Embodied signals in supervision

Whether meeting in person or on screen, effective supervisors will be 'hearing' the body speak from minute one of the session. The sadness or excitement in the eyes as the supervisee arrives. The nervous chatter as they hang up their coat or adjust the camera online. The rise and fall in energy as the session unfolds. This is all material for noticing and wondering. Julie Joseph reflects:

> My supervisee arrives in their room, the screen between us. I am struck by how fast they speak, how they are constantly moving even when seated. Clothes being rearranged, hands picking at threads, head moving quickly from side to side, the lack of meeting of our eyes, the sense of distraction. I become aware of the unsettledness this brings into my body.
>
> I mirror this back and offer kinaesthetic attunement by saying how restless they seem. How that feels in me, my heart speeding up, by stomach constricting, the muscles of my face held in a tight mask. My shoulders feeling tense. As if I am ready for flight, to run, to react quickly to anything. I explain I feel exhausted already.
>
> And we meet. We meet eyes, they stop and pay attention internally to themselves. I offer my active body for them to observe and model. I take a deep breath, slowly exhale, I drop my shoulders, I hold their gaze. I relax into my chair and I pause.
>
> Welcome to supervision. Here I am, here you are. I see you, I'm with you, I'm like you. You are welcome.[72]

---

[72] Julie Joseph OBE, Movement Psychotherapist and Supervisor

Embodied forms of exploring

The invitation to embodied exploration may arise in response to a variety of phenomena: feelings; images; concepts; impulses. *Feelings*: 'I feel so thrilled to be offered this opportunity'; *Images*: 'I am at rock bottom at work right now'; *Concepts*: 'I need to put on my big boy pants and just get on and do it'; *Body impulse*: 'I am just itching to move on from this.' Anyone of these could be the launching pad for embodied exploration through movement.

Supervisors who are paying attention will sometimes hear hints in the way supervisees present things that offer the possibility of embodied exploration.

I've got this awful situation at work. I think I've been carrying it for weeks.

'Where are you carrying it?' .. 'How much does it weigh?'..

'This room is full of things. I wonder if you would be willing to find something that feels like the weight of this thing you have been carrying around for weeks.'

Notice in this example that the supervisor does not need to know what the 'thing' is. The supervisee has that information already and supervision is not information exchange. The invitation to help the supervisee explore the weight he is carrying is a form of paying very close attention not just to the story line but to the manner in which the supervisee has presented it. Either way 'carrying' is an embodied action which the supervisor can pick up on.

Other clues are given in action words.

> 'Everything is just out of reach … not far but just out of reach'

I wonder if you could show me that reaching in your body? What did you notice? Where does that take you?

The Embodied Supervisor - Somatic Resonance

One of the ways in which embodiment can be integrated into supervision is for the supervisor to notice what happens within them as the supervisee presents their material. 'What is not transformed is likely to be transferred. And what is not owned may well be thrown.'

Supervisors who are grounded, ready and available for whatever comes into the supervisory space, may experience material which has not been fully owned by their supervisees or by those involved in the material they are exploring. This phenomena know as somatic resonance, is a form of 'communication by impact': such experiences often suggest that something or some dynamic has become homeless. Eager to resolve its sorry state it takes up residence in the first person who will let it in. Often that person is the supervisor. Common forms of somatic resonance include:

feelings of hunger which were not there before the supervision began; a sense of the body shrinking or disappearing at some point in the session that was not there before; a stitch in the side; a crook in the neck; a sudden inability to hold your head up; the feeling that your eyelids will close any moment. If such phenomena had been given a home they would not be floating in the air waiting to land on the most susceptible person available. Supervisors who experience somatic resonance of this kind should be assured that such awareness is not a distraction but rather an incisive and acutely focused invitation to help something which is homeless find a home, something which is free floating to find a resting place.

How supervisors share embodied information of this kind with their supervisees will depend on a number of factors: the balance between power and vulnerability in the relationship; the reflexive capacity of the supervisee to work effectively with unconscious phenomenon; the developmental stage of the supervisee etc. With a novice practitioner with little experience, a supervisor who is experiencing hunger arising during a session might simply say: 'I wonder whether you are looking for something that you haven't found yet' whereas with an experienced practitioner she might say 'I am getting a sense of hunger here, does that resonate with you?'.

Exploring the Felt Sense

The 'felt sense' is 'the unclear, pre-verbal sense of something we experience in the body. It is not the same as an emotion, but rather a bodily sense of the *total* situation'.[73] Feeling something in our guts, precedes cognitive thought, reason or reflection. The father of Focusing E.T. Gendlin offers the following six stage process which could be used in supervision to deepen and explore the felt sense of things.

Focusing Exercise

Allow yourself to focus on some aspect of your work.

Relaxing – Ask your body 'How am I?' with that aspect of my work.

Felt sense – What is your felt sense of the situation you have identified? – spend time there exploring and asking questions of it.

Handle – listen for the words, phrases or images which emerge from the felt sense.

Resonating – Experiment with words, phrases or images until you find a fit between them and the felt sense.

Asking – ask the felt sense what it is and what it might need.

Receiving – receive whatever happens in a kindly way.[74]

---

[73] Taiwo Afuape Bowan
[74] E. T. Gendlin (2003) in Bownas and Fredman, 102

To follow up

Bloom, K. (2006) *The Embodied Self,* London: Karnac Books.

Bownas, J. and Fredman, G. (2017) *Working with Embodiment in Supervision: A systemic approach,* London: Routledge.

Butté, C. (2013, Embodiment and Movement in Supervision in Chesner and Zografou *Creative Supervision Across Modalities,* London: Jessica Kingsley 127-44.

Payne, H. (2008) *Supervision of Dance Movement Psychotherapy: A Practitioner's Handbook,* London: Routledge

Online Resources

A myriad of body stilling exercises breathing exercises, guided visualisations, body scans can be found online.

Double breathing is a very effective way of grounding the body. Inhale through the nose with a short, sharp inhalation followed directly by a long, strong inhale. Then without pausing, exhale through the nose and mouth with a short, then long exhale. Repeat 3 times.

Scottish Ballet has created movement and breath sessions for health and social care staff to help them deal with the stresses of Covid-19. A selection of ten minute sessions is available at www.scottishballet.co.uk/health-at-hand

For those who wish to take this further, the Therapeutic Art of Movement Institute runs training and continuing professional development workshops. http://taomi.tilda.ws

Two women walked

Two women walked the road
And as they walked
they talked -
of death and resurrection
of hope and promise
of faith and discernment
of love and discipleship
Sharing a vocation
that is costly and demanding
Sifting through the detritus
for the jewels that are buried.
And between them
was the risen Christ
listening and encouraging
consoling and affirming
making his presence known
in the breaking of the bread of life
- the sharing of stories
of joys and disappointments
of comfort and longings
Souls laid bare
not seeking answers
or solutions

not even congratulations
or commiserations
But simply the sacred gift
of listening
in which the work of healing is begun.[75]

~ Liz Crumlish

---

[75] This emerged from reflecting on the story of Jesus walking with the two disciples on the Road to Emmaus in Luke 24:13-35.

Drama & Role

Role is a core concept in creative supervision. According to the father of role theory, Jacob L. Moreno, 'role is the functioning form the individual takes in any moment.'[76] In everyday speech, we associate 'playing a role' with 'falseness and inauthenticity' but that is not what we mean when we speak of working with role in supervision.[77]

Each of us has a role repertoire. Some roles are over developed, others are underdeveloped. As wholehearted committed practitioners, many caring professionals (supervisors included) have an overdeveloped caring role to which they readily default. 'Something needs done, I'll do it'. 'Things have gone pear shaped, I'll try and fix them.' 'Feathers are ruffled, I'll smooth things over.' Those with overdeveloped restorative roles are likely to wear themselves out. Such people may well have underdeveloped roles around being appropriately assertive, challenging injustice or confronting root causes.

Helping a person recognise their overdeveloped and underdeveloped roles and encouraging them to broaden their role repertoire is an invaluable aspect of supervision. Life experiences often result in people being 'rigidly attached to the roles [they] are familiar with and avoidant of those new situations that make new role demands.'[78] For

---

[76] Cited in Chesner and Zografou (2014) 43.
[77] cf the world of Robert Landy on role theory and role methods eg. (1991) Taxonomy of Roles, *The Arts in Psychotherapy*, 18:5
[78] Anna Chesner, in Chesner and Zografou,(2014) *Creative Supervision Across Modalities*, London: Jessica Kingsley 46.

example the adult child of an alcoholic or emotionally absent parent may have learned from an early age to do whatever they can to keep the family together. Similarly the adult child of warring parents may have an overdeveloped role as peacekeeper which results in the avoidance of conflict in adult life.

Role repertoire is as relevant to supervisors as it is to supervisees. Antony Williams identifies four roles for the supervisor: Facilitator, Teacher, Evaluator and Consultant.[79]

As a facilitator the role of the supervisor is to host and contain, to elicit a focus and to enable exploration of the supervisee's material. As a teacher, the formative role is to enable the supervisee to learn by offering coaching, expanding understanding and extending skills. As an evaluator, the role of the supervisor is to weigh things up through tracking and monitoring such that an appropriate modality of exploration may be proposed which meets the supervisees' developmental stage, processing style and contextual obligations. As a consultant, the role of supervisor is to make their wisdom and experience available when the supervisee requests it.

Most supervisors will be more comfortable in one of these roles than others. The same is true for supervisees. A practitioner who needs to be every client's friend may avoid the evaluator role and struggle to offer constructive feedback/feedforward comments or write evaluative reports. Likewise a practitioner with years of experience may resist creative modalities such as the Inner Wise Guide (see p 171) since the facilitation of that process leaves no

---

[79] Anthony Williams (1995) *Visual and Active supervision: Roles, Focus, Technique*, New York, London: Norton

room whatsoever for the supervisor's wisdom to be displayed.

Role Reversal

Role reversal is a key therapeutic technique which can be effectively used to gain insight into other people's perspectives. In supervision it can be used to gain greater understanding of how others may perceive situations and dynamics that arise in supervision.

> **Role Reversal**
>
> 'I wonder if we could explore this in action rather than in words?' I ask. With Zak's agreement I invite him to find a space in the room where he can 'be' Deb (his colleague with whom he is in conflict).
>
> Zak chooses a seat near the door and sits down. I invite him to settle into that space and imagine how it is to be Deb: to assume her posture, her way of being in the world, her demeanour. I am not asking him to 'become' Deb but to get a felt sense of how it is to live life in her shoes.
>
> I invite Zak to tell me three things about Deb. 'What are you wearing?' 'What do you do at break times?' 'What matters to you?'

> As Zak becomes more established in the role of Deb I ask about Zak. Tell me three things about your colleague Zak. Anything at all.
>
> I listen but say nothing.
>
> 'Zak says he is in dispute with you. I wonder how that is for you?'
>
> I listen but say nothing.
>
> Once 'Deb' has spoken, I invite Zak to come back to his original seat in the room, to de-role 'Deb' and to speak as Zak, as himself. From that place of his own identity (ie no longer in role), I invite him to reflect on what has happened.
>
> What did he notice from getting into Deb's shoes?
>
> What did he notice in what she said about him?
>
> What did he notice in how she spoke of the dispute between them?
>
> Where is he now with his supervisory question?

Role reversal offers a felt sense of how things may be perceived by other(s) in the story. It also offers feedback from those who witness it. In individual supervision this will be the supervisor. 'I noticed when asked to locate Deb in the room you became restless and were constantly in motion.' Witnesses are not interpreters. Witnesses feedback what they see. They do not interpret the meaning of what they see. Once again the three levels of seeing provide an economic and safe way to open things up in supervision rather than prematurely close them down. 'I wonder how it was for you to hear Deb speak of you as she did?' has the potential to open things up whereas 'you really need to listen to what Deb said about you if you are ever going to be able to work with her' closes things down. In group supervision the group members offer a more expansive 'cloud of witnesses'[80] who will see, hear, feel and sense an even wider range of things which may be gently offered back to the supervisee.

Given the impact that role reversal can have it is very important to de-role those who have taken part before moving on in the session. One way of doing this is to invite those who have played a role in the session to return to their original places in the room, adopt their own body postures and to say something about themselves which helps to ground them. For example 'I am not Deb. I am Zak. I have a wife and kids at home. I will be going to the canteen for lunch. After work today I will be playing five a sides.' Speaking from the 'I' rather than from the adopted role helps supervisees disentangle what belongs to them and what belongs to other people. In group supervision in which people have played 'borrowed' roles in scenarios which are charged with emotion or tricky dynamics it can be helpful to invite them to physically shake off the role and speak

---

[80] Hebrews 12.1

aloud as appropriate. 'I am not a nasty boss. I am not someone who never listens. I am not dead inside. My name is Jane. I love being a social worker. I am utterly committed to the kids I am trying to place. I have great relationships with my colleagues'.

Working with parts of the self

As we saw earlier, internal conflicts are common in supervision and offer profitable opportunities for creative exploration. 'On the one hand I could … on the other …' When supervisees present with choices, supervisors can facilitate the externalisation of their internalised dramas not only through projective methods such as choosing cloths or objects symbolising each option, but also through inviting the supervisee to take an embodied stance using chairs or cushions. An example:

Freya comes to supervision with this dilemma.

> 'I am 65 and have one year to go before I get my state pension. In 12 months I could retire completely. Or I could cut down my hours to part-time and only work mornings. Or I could go on working while I have the energy and health to do so. I just can't work out which to choose from.'

I invite Freya to explore through a combination of embodiment and role work using the chair method.

> **Chair work in Supervision**
>
> Since you have three options I wonder if you could choose three chairs in the room, one for each option. 'I am in my dining room' she says 'so that's easy'.
>
> I invite her to choose a chair which represents retiring completely in 12 months.
>
> I invite you to settle into that chair and imagine yourself a week into having retired completely. What comes to awareness from that place? (I encourage her to use sentences beginning with 'I'.)
>
> When she comes to a natural stop I invite her to leave that chair and choose another chair to explore her second option and so on until she has tried all three chairs.
>
> I then invite her to move to another space in the room from which she can see all three chairs. From that observing stance I ask what was stirred within her.
>
> I then invite Freya back to her original chair in the supervisory space.
>
> I ask her to say where she is now with her supervisory issue.

Supervision in this modality allows for the rehearsal, improvisation and re-scripting of dramas which arise in practitioners' lives. Thankfully not everything that comes to supervision is 'dramatic' in the popular sense of the word, but every work-based story has a plot, characters, scenery, lines spoken and unspoken and endings of various kinds. Often what we are doing in supervision is enabling supervisees to 'bring out [their] internal drama so that the drama within becomes the drama outside'.[81] If everyone lived happily ever after, supervisors would be redundant!

Supervision and Experimentation

> 'Through spontaneity we are re-formed into ourselves. [Spontaneity] creates an explosion that for the moment frees us from handed-down frames of reference, memory choked with old facts and information and undigested theories and techniques of other people's findings. Spontaneity is the moment of personal freedom when we are faced with reality, and see it, explore it and act accordingly. In this reality the bits and pieces of ourselves function as an organic whole. It is the time of discovery, of experiencing, of creative expression.'[82]

---

[81] Karp, M., Holmes, P., and Bradshaw Tauvon, K. Eds. (1998) *The Handbook of Psychodrama*, London: Routledge

[82] Viola Spolin (1963) *Improvisation for the Theater: A Handbook of Teaching and Directing Techniques*. Evanston, IL: Northwestern University Press, 4.

One of the most useful aspects of supervision is the opportunity it affords to get behind the scenes and ask 'what was really going on?' 'what part did each character play?' 'What is my part in this unfolding drama?' 'Is the script set in stone or have I room for improvisation?'

> 'I wanted to explore what happened when I suggested our team take on a new project. It didn't go the way I had hoped. I wonder if I missed something'

Such scenarios in which someone wants to check out what they have done are fairly common in supervision. Sometimes they are presented in black and white terms: 'Did I get it right?' or 'Where did I go wrong?' Effective supervisors will know that they have no authority to answer such questions and that to do so is not in the supervisee's best interests. Much more effective is to help supervisees explore what lies beneath the question. 'What is about that issue that still tugs at your mind or your heart?' 'What is it about what happened that you would like to explore here?'

This kind of exploration favours supervision as experimentation. When supervision happens in a group setting the option always exists for the supervisee to 'use' group members in the re-presentation of the situation. Assigning group members to specific roles (colleagues A, B and C) can offer the supervisee the chance to replay what happened in the original situation from various angles. For example participants could be asked how it was to be cast in each role.

> 'I felt so cut off from my colleagues. I wanted to be allowed to stand with them and didn't like being positioned across a desk.'

> 'I just zoned out'.

> 'I so wanted to help but those two just were not up for it.'

Having heard such responses from each participant the supervisor can ask the supervisee whether anything resonates with them. The issue is not to re-enact what CCTV would have shown happened in the original situation. The original situation is done and dusted. The focus in supervision is on the impact the situation had on the supervisee and any ongoing consequences which result from it.

The relationship a practitioner has to a past event may also be explored by experimenting with different next steps or endings. 'I wish I had said X' says the supervisee. 'Then try saying it hear' says the supervisor 'and see what it does for you.'

Inner Wise Guide Modality

The Inner Wise Guide modality is based on three things: i) the conviction that supervisees are wise ii) that immediate access to that wisdom is sometimes not available and iii) that the supervisee's own inner wisdom is more likely to be transformative than the 'wisdom' a supervisor imparts. This dramatic form of supervision requires the supervisor to offer strong hosting and containment since it frequently uncovers deep material.

While narrative forms of supervision engage the supervisor and supervisee in conversation, this modality casts the supervisor as a stage director who gives very clear directions and whose primary role is to facilitate an internal dialogue within the supervisee. Minimal output for maximum impact is what is required from the supervisor.

The modality invites the supervisee to find a Wise Guide who knows their way around the issue being explored. That Wise Guide could be a real person living or dead, a character from a fairy tale, film, book, historical or fictional. In eliciting a Wise Guide, supervisors need to practice restraint in not permitting their own knowledge or experience of the chosen person to colour the session. My 'Snow White' and your 'Snow White' may not be the same person. Yours may be the epitome of feminine innocence and kindness. Mine may be the victim of misogynistic patriarchal oppression.

Key to the stage directing role of the supervisor in this modality, is that they avoid engaging the supervisee in discussion, explanation or self-justification. As a pared down form of supervision, supervisors who use the Inner Wise Guide should not try to understand supervisees but rather simply trust that the issue brought and the Guide identified has meaning for them.[83]

---

[83] This is a form of listening for what ignites and what extinguishes rather than supervision as information exchange cf Nancy Kline (1999) *Time to Think: Listening to Ignite The Human Mind*, London: Cassell.

Inner Wise Guide

Invite the supervisee to take a moment to arrive in the space. (Hosting & Containing)

Invite the supervisee to name something they want to bring to supervision. (Eliciting & Focusing)

What would you like to explore in our time together today?

Invite supervisee to say why they are bringing that issue to supervision today. (Eliciting & Focusing)

'Who in your world could help them with this?. Let your imagination run freely. It could be absolutely anyone: living or dead; historical or imaginary character; someone from a story or film.

Tell me three things about the person you have chosen.

Ask what struck them from what the Wise Guide said or did. What insights (if any) they have gained? Is there anything they now want to pursue. (Tracking & Monitoring)

Invite supervisee to name what they will take from this supervision session. (Bridging & Enacting) [84]

---

[84] Adapted from material in Leach & Paterson, (2015) *Pastoral Supervision: A Handbook*, 182-84.

Body Sculpting

Creating body sculpts can be a very powerful and embodied way of discovering one's true feelings about something or someone.

> 'Could you choose a posture to indicate how it is for you to work in that team?'

> Could you choose a posture to indicate your response to your client?

The sculpts could be amplified by inviting the supervisee to speak out of the sculpt.

> 'As you wedge yourself between the door and the wall, what feelings arise?'

> 'If the sculpt could speak what would it say?'

Sculpts can be further amplified by the supervisor 'doubling' it, that is by the supervisor adopting a similar posture such that the supervisee can see themselves with the observer's eye.

Dramatized forms of Bridging and Enacting

During the Coronavirus pandemic, a healthcare worker described her ritual for ending her day at work. She would drive home, enter by the back door, change in her utility room, placing the clothes she was wearing straight into the washing machine. She would then take a shower and dress in fresh clothes before she greeted her family. That ritual provided a transition between work and family life, a liminal space in which she could leave one behind to enter the other.

Supervision might be considered a liminal space, where one arrives with one premise and leaves with another. However transition is encountered in supervision, whether by narrative, by creative play, by role reversal or some other modality, bridging and enacting may be enhanced by considering the use of tokens of transition – some element, physical or metaphorical that enables the supervisee to retain something of the realisation that was theirs in supervision. This might be a photograph of the installation they have created. It could be a phrase written on a Post-It note that they place somewhere that they will encounter it frequently. It may be a ritual that they choose to engage in, such as shaking the dust from their feet or having a bonfire. Whatever is chosen, it is a way of not losing touch with the insight they have gained.

To follow up

Chesner, A. (2013) 'Role as a Core Concept in Creative Supervision' in Chesner and Zografou, *Creative Supervision Across Modalities*, London: Jessica Kingsley

Ford, D. (2009) 'Are you able to drink the cup that I drink?' A Reflection on the Significance of Pastoral Supervision in Health Care Chaplaincy, *Practical Theology* 2.3, 343-354.

Ionadidou, E. (2013) The Psychodrama of Supervision, in Chesner, A. and Zografou, *Creative Supervision Across Modalities*, London: Jessica Kingsley

Jones, P. and Ditty Dokter, D. (2008) *Supervision of Dramatherapy*, London: Routledge

Moreno, J. L. (1987b). The Role Concept: A Bridge Between Psychiatry and Sociology. In J. Fox (Ed.) *The Essential Moreno*, New York: Springer.

When periphery becomes central stage

Reflecting on the healing of the woman who touched the hem of Jesus' garment. Matthew 9:20-22

On his way elsewhere
at the edge of his vision
a woman took her chances,
reached out to touch him
and stopped him in his tracks.
Though his course was set
his intention clear
still he made space
for the unforeseen
noticing the unexpressed
bringing front and centre
the courage mustered
and naming the faith enacted.
Displaying compassion
calling forth wisdom
and pride
rewarding the risk taken
honouring the meeting of souls
that happens on the edges
yet, when afforded space
makes healing a possibility.
A peripheral encounter
becomes centre stage.

~ Liz Crumlish

Language & Story

The words supervisees use in bringing material to supervision are often pregnant with meaning and provide the supervisor with a sense of the weight, size, scale and significance of the presenting issue. Very often the kernel of the issues that supervisees want to explore are given in their opening sentences.

> 'I think I might be on thin ice here but I just cannot accept what the new management are asking of us.'

'Thin ice' is an evocative image. Catching the phrase before it gets lost under a whole lot of other words could be illuminating. Pausing sufficiently to permit such language to be heard, slows the session down creating the kind of spaciousness which enables supervisees to explore things more deeply.

> 'Tell me about that ice. What do you see? Describe it to me?'
>
> 'Where are you viewing that ice from?'
>
> 'Just how thin is it?'
>
> 'Do you know your way around ice?'
>
> ''What do you think would happen if you stay on the ice?'
>
> 'Is staying on thin ice the only option open to you?'

Paying such close attention to the language supervisees use needs to be done with caution. The aim is to help supervisee's track themselves not to cause them to retreat into self-conscious censorship or reduce them to silence.

> 'I am surprised to find that the ice is not that thin and I can skate better than I thought I could'.
>
> 'And where does that take you with the issue you brought to supervision today?'
>
> 'It leaves me less anxious to speak up.'

Clean Language

Having watched therapists at work and having analysed transcripts of their sessions, David Grove realised just how often therapists subtly changed what clients actually said and how those changes distanced clients from their experiences. He developed the concept of Clean Language to enable helping professionals stay closer to what was actually happening for their clients rather than to pursue lines of enquiry based on what they thought was happening.

As an extension of Clean Language, Grove proposed an approach called Clean Questions in which fewer presuppositions are made. When supervisors asks supervisees 'What are you thinking?' the question already presupposes that supervisees are indeed thinking. But they may not be! 'Cleaning' the question, he suggests supervisors asks: 'Are you thinking anything?' or if they want to be super-clean: 'Is there anything else about … ?'

> **Clean Language**
>
> Is there anything else about that … ?
> What kind of … is that … ?
> Where is … ?
> Whereabouts … ?
> That's … like what?
> How many … are there?
>
> Is there are relationship between … and … ?
> Is … the same or different to … ?
> Is … on the inside or the outside?
>
> If the supervisee is talking about something which happens additional questions might be
>
> Then what happens?
> What happens next?
> What happens just before … ?
> What would you like to have happen?
> What needs to happen for … to happen?
> When … what happens to … ?

Tracking language is a form of tracking insight. The more supervisors engage in verbosity the less supervisees will be able to 'hear themselves out' in the language and metaphors they use. Staying as close to that language as possible allows supervisees to mine it for meaning until they find what they are looking for.

> 'I used that expression 'thin ice' as a throwaway line. It hadn't been in my head until we started speaking but I can't believe just how apt it was. I had been thinking that the only option I had

was to do nothing since speaking up at work would result in the ice cracking and me sinking into a watery grave. But that's not how I see it now.'

The point of clean language is to acknowledge

i) what the supervisee has said (freed from the supervisor's interpretations);

ii) to help the supervisee zoom in and focus on an aspect of the supervisory issue which has meaning for them and

iii) to facilitate the supervisee's quest for self-knowledge (rather than supervisor-focused wisdom or validation).[85]

Language in Eliciting and Focusing

Catching the metaphors and images that people use, especially the things that are said right at the beginning of a session can help elicit a focus early on leaving the bulk of the time for exploration. Throwaway lines or metaphors can carry meaning. They are worthy of investigation. Words are impactful both for the speaker and the listener.[86] Listening in stereo with one ear to the words the supervisee uses and another ear to the impact those words have on the supervisor can open a world of inquiry for supervisees. Take for example a supervisee in residential childcare who begins a session saying:

---

[85] For more on Clean Language see Lawley, J. & Manea, A.I. (2017). 'The Use of Clean Space to Facilitate a 'Stuck' Client: a Case Study', *Journal of Experiential Psychotherapy*, 20(4):62–70.
[86] Cf Glenda Fredman in Bownas and Fredman, (2017), 64.

> 'I love working with the kids. But I hate the endless meetings we have every week. They are such a waste of time'.

Listening in mono the supervisor could respond with a question intended to ease the transition from generalisation to distillation:

> 'You say you love the kids, but what exactly do you love about that work?'

Or the supervisor could focus in on the comment that meetings are a waste of time.

> 'What is it about those meetings that make it a waste of time?'
>
> Or 'What part do you play in those meetings?'
>
> 'Have you ever spoken up and said how you feel about those meetings?'
>
> How do you contribute to making those meetings a waste of time'
>
> or 'What are you willing to do to make those meetings more meaningful?'

Listening in stereo occurs when supervisors hear what is said about the then and there of the work space as possibly also relevant within the supervisory space. Listening in stereo, a supervisor might say to the supervisee: 'you say you hate endless meetings and yet you and are I having a work based meeting right now, I wonder if it will be a waste of time?' or: 'What would it take for this work based meeting not to be a waste of time?' or 'What would make this meeting worthwhile for you?' Or again, 'What part are you willing to play to ensure this meeting is not a waste of time?'

> **Six Minute Journaling**
>
> Six Minute Journaling (or freewriting) is an impactful way of distillation in which the focus for supervision can emerge. It can be used when people do not know what to bring to supervision or when their heads are full.
>
> Key to the process is providing a few carefully chosen words with which to begin eg.
>
> 'The thing about work right now is …'
> 'Today will be worthwhile if …'
> 'The itch in my practice is …'
> 'The change I would love to implement is …'
>
> Invite supervisees to write or type for six minutes without editing or erasing what they have written.
>
> At the end of the six minutes invite them to read it over and then circle 3 or 4 key words.
>
> Finally invite supervisees to give the story a title as if it were a book or a film.
>
> The session could continue by exploring the title.

Ink polaroids for Eliciting a Focus

Long before mobile phones were commonplace the nearest people could get to instant photography was polaroid prints. Stuart David of the Scottish indie band *Belle and Sebastian* writes: 'It used to be I had a camera called a Zenit but now I just take photographs with a cheap old pen.' David's 'ink polaroids' are short texts capturing his band at work, at rest and at play.[87] Being concise and economic with language, ink polaroids can be a very effective way of eliciting a focus at the start of a supervision session.

'If you were to think of your work since we last met, what polaroids would you create to capture the key features?'

Writing a way into Supervision

I saw Kara from the window when I looked out between appointments – she looked weighed down.

'What's in your backpack?' I asked as I invited her in.

'Good question,' she answered – and I knew that, already, our supervision session had begun.

'I need to explore whether I want to re-invent myself in my current role, or whether it's time to move on'

'How would you like to do that?'

---

[87] Stuart David (1997) *Ink Polaroids of Belle and Sebastian*. I am grateful to IPSRP graduate Sarah Heywood for bringing this to my attention.

'I want to write' she said – 'using that prompt you just gave me: What's in your backpack?'

Kara rifled through her backpack for a moment and then began writing. Within 10 minutes she asked if she could read what she had written.

> I carry my faith in a backpack:
> overflowing with:
> pencils
> permanent markers
> post-it notes
> sticky tape
> blu-tac
> a cable or three
> water bottle
> coffee mug
> hand cream
> contact lens solution
> batteries
> trainers

I asked her: 'Is there anything you want to add or underline?'

A few minutes later, she read her reflection out loud again:

> I carry my faith in a backpack:
> overflowing with:
> pencils – the kind with erasers on the end – so I can rub things out
> permanent markers – for important, not to be erased, memories
> post-it notes – to carry reminders, keeping them in view
> sticky tape
> blu-tac

a cable or three – for all sorts of connections
water bottle
coffee mug
hand cream
contact lens solution
batteries
trainers

'Where does that take you?', I asked. 'I'm not entirely sure' she said, 'but that's enough today. I'd like to take this away and work with it.' 'OK' I said, slightly bemused, but recognising that Kara had got all she needed for today. We arranged our next session and Kara left.

As I greeted Kara in our next session, I noticed she looked a lot lighter. She still had her backpack but it didn't seem to be weighing her down so much. Once again, with little preamble, Kara said: 'I want to share something I wrote after our last session.'

> Time to unpack. There is so much stuff in my overflowing backpack that I refuse to carry around any longer.
> So I am jettisoning the post-it notes that remind me of things it's time to forget.
> I'm discarding the sticky tape and blu-tac that keep me stuck where I am.
> I'll hang on to the pencils with their erasers but dump the permanent markers.
> And the cables have to go – a freer connection seems possible.
> And, I'm kicking off the trainers and donning sharp stilettos that will certainly leave their mark.
> I'll need the hand cream to bring some balm when the dirty work is done.

And so began a session in which Kara reflected on her process and her realisation that it was time for her to move out of her current professional role and embrace a new opportunity unencumbered by the weight she had carried.

My part in it all? To create a hospitable space big enough for Kara to sift through her backpack as she did the work of noticing and wondering and to bear witness as she realised where her insight was taking her. Having someone to hold space and bear witness is worth its weight in gold as even the most self-directing of supervisees needs to be accompanied .

Language in Exploring and Imagining

In *When women were birds: Fifty Four variations on Voice*', Terry Tempest Williams writes 'we don't find our voice, our voice finds us.'[88] The following guidance would serve supervisees well in exploring the material they have brought to supervision.

---

[88] Terry Tempest Williams (2013) *When women were birds: Fifty Four variations on Voice,* New York: Picador, 37. With thanks to IPSRP graduate Alison Ransome for introducing me to this wonderful book.

Write in pencil

Write in pencil …
The permanence of ink is an illusion.
Ink fades and is absorbed into the paper.
Water can smear it.
Ink runs out.
A pencil can be sharpened repeatedly
And then disappear in the process.
Like me.[89]

Write a word.
Not the right word.
Turn the pencil upside down, erase.
Back and forth on the page.
Pencil upright.
Begin again.
Point on the page.
Pause.
Find the right word.
Write the word.
Word by word,
the language of women
so often begins with a whisper.[90]

~ Terry Tempest Williams

---

[89] Tempest Williams, (2013) 21
[90] Tempest Williams, (2013) 23

Writing a different ending

During his time in Auschwitz, Viktor Frankl discovered his freedom. He writes:

> The experiences of camp life show that humanity does have a choice of action. ... We who lived in concentration camps can remember the people who walked through the huts comforting others, giving away their last piece of bread. They may have been few in number, but they offer sufficient proof that everything can be taken from a person but one thing: the last of the human freedoms—to choose one's attitude in any given set of circumstances, to choose one's own way. . . . When we are no longer able to change a situation . . . we are challenged to change ourselves. Between stimulus and response there is a space. In that space is our power to choose our response. In our response lies our growth and our freedom.[91]

One way of exploring in supervision is for supervisees to be invited to imagine a different ending to their story, an ending which may not necessarily change the situation but which challenges them to change something about themselves. An ending which allows their values and ultimately their soul not to be extinguished.

---

[91] Viktor E. Frankl, *Man's Search for Meaning* (Beacon Press: 1959, 2006), 65–67, 112.

Language in Tracking & Monitoring

Many supervisors, especially those who are trained in therapeutic listening, have been programmed to believe that it is their task to understand what supervisees are saying and that the more they understand, the more helpful they will be. Nancy Kline challenges this and suggests that it is not the act of being understood that changes things so much as having our passions ignited and being able to identify whatever threatens to extinguish them. The consequence for supervisors is that they need worry less about content and detail and more about energy and inquiry. A simple way of tracking in supervision is to ask supervisees questions like:

Tracking through language

'Of all the things you have heard yourself say today, what is the most important for you right now?'

'Of all the feelings that have arisen in this session, what are you most in touch with right now?'

'Of all that has gone through your mind as we have been exploring this, what grabs your attention right now?'

Tracking of this kind relieves supervisors from having to try and remember every detail of the session. It also relieves them of having to feedback back verbatim what was said. Tracking then becomes something that supervisees do for themselves rather than something that supervisors do for them. When supervisees track their own process of inquiry they provide a steer or directive for their supervisor sto pick up and follow.

Wordles for Tracking & Monitoring

Another way of tracking the journey from issue to insight in supervision is to ask supervisees: 'If all the words we have been using today were fed into a wordle what word(s) would stand out? '

Language in Bridging & Enacting

Bridging and enacting is all about capturing the insights that have been discovered in supervision. If action is to follow, then such insights need to be focused and memorable. The fewer the words the better.

Bridging & Enacting

'What tweet would sum up what you have found today?'

'If today's session had a #hashtag, what would it say?'

'If you were to share your new found insight on Instagram what would you post?'

Language in Reviewing & Closing

Reviewing and closing does what it says on the tin. Supervisors who ask in the closing moments 'is there anything else you wanted to look at today?' are acting irresponsibly since time will not allow such exploration. Reviewing can take a number of forms:

Reviewing & Closing

'As you look back over the session what do you notice about yourself, about the issue your brought,
or about how we worked together?'

'What was helpful/unhelpful in the way we worked today?'

'As we go forward is there anything you would like more of/less of from our work together?'

Exploring Story

> 'One is never cured of memory. That is why one writes. . . . Today at last I have to find the words to write the narrative of my life. I have the right, after all, to choose how to narrate myself, even if I did not choose the story.'   Ahl am Mosteghanemi [92]

In bygone days, every Scottish community had a Seanchaidh, a bearer of stories, who passed on, from generation to generation, the rich history and tradition of a culture. Sometimes their art was downplayed as a good evening's entertainment, recounting tales that provoked mirth and fear in equal measure. But the reach and purpose of the Seanchaidh drilled much deeper, provoking insight and wisdom that transcended the passage of time, preserving the very root of the community's psyche. The Seanchaidh was able to incisively name what she saw, to call it out, alerting attention and leaving interpretation open. The task of the Seanchaidh was to remain curious, leaving judgment for others.

What if that same curiosity and calling out were employed in supervision, wrestling with stories that afford insight and preserving the task of making meaning for those to whom it belongs? How might we share our stories, attending to what we see, responding to what we feel and embodying the sense-making we find?

There is something non-threatening about a story well told or well written that makes room for both the hearer and the teller to inhabit.

---

[92] Ahl am Mosteghanemi, *Dhakirat al-jasad*, Beirut: Dar al-adab, 1998), 9.

Bringing Stories to Supervision

Supervisees can be invited to bring stories: stories from children's story books, from novels in which they recognise themselves or in which a plot carries echoes of personal experience. Supervisees can also be encouraged to engage in their own creative writing and to use it as a medium with which to explore the soul of their work and the dynamics which are played out in their professional relationships and environment.

Using stories in supervision can be particularly useful when offering group supervision to people who work together in the same organisation. Exploring supervisory issues through the medium of a story can offer a measure of safety and anonymity which may not otherwise be possible by straight narration of the issue. Participants can grapple with stories in a less inhibited way than might otherwise be possible and, as perceptions are realised, less helpful dynamics may be challenged and healthier relationships forged.

Working with Story in Supervision

The brevity of children's stories many of which are produced pictorially provide a rich repertoire for exploration in supervision. They can be read aloud in the session or watched online. Here a few that supervisees have found useful.

Stories for Use in Supervision
Stuck by Oliver Jeffers
The Giving Tree by Shiel Silverstein
Tina the Tree by Andrew McDonough

The Rabbit Listened by Cori Doerrfeld
The Bear and the Piano by David Litchfield
The Boy, Mole, Fox and Horse by Charlie Mackesy

One way of engaging with a story heard or watched on a shared screen online comes from the practice of Mindfulness.

Engaging with Story

Encouraging
Invite supervisees to say what they notice in themselves as the story was told: physical sensations; emotions; thoughts.

Dialoguing
Invite supervisees to dialogue with what happened as the story was told: What was familiar? surprising?; Were there any echoes from their own lives or experience?; Did any words, phrases, resonate?

Linking
How does what has arisen relate to the supervisory issue brought today?

Centre for Mindfulness Practice[93]

---

[93] Centre for Mindfulness Research & Practice, Bangor University (2012) *Teacher Training Retreat for Mindfulness-based Teacher: Resource Pack*, Bangor, Wales

Writing Stories in Supervision

According to Maya Angelou, 'there is no greater agony than bearing an untold story inside you.'[94] As a projective method of hearing ourselves into speech, writing has a significant role to play in 'hearing ourselves out' in supervision. Liz Crumlish writes:

> 'In a creative writing workshop in which I participated, writers were encouraged to engage with Scripture, to read into the text and draw out of the text their contemporary weaving. In a subsequent sharing of that interpolative exercise in a supervisory space, the noticing, wondering and holding of a peer supervisor enabled me to realise profound insight.'[95]

She offers one such interpolation based on the biblical story of Sarah laughing when she was told that at her great age she would conceive and bear a son.[96]

Why did Sarah laugh?
NOT - as some would have us believe
because she lacked faith
NOR out of the sheer joy at the prospect
of resurrecting her beloved's sexual prowess
(she believed in miracles after all)
Not even at the absurdity of being 90 and pregnant!
Sarah laughed
because all through this patriarchal narrative

---

[94] Maya Angelou (1969) *I Know Why the Caged Bird Sings*, New York: Random House
[95] Personal correspondence. Used with permission.
[96] Genesis 18:9-12

when she was moved from pillar to post
continually used and abused
her body touted as a guaranty and token
at the whim of men playing power games
it was hilarious that her body
should call their bluff
carrying within it
the seed of a nation
Sarah laughed as a warning:
Be careful what you wish for
A woman's body
will not be diminished
will not succumb
to the flagrant disregard of men
and their games of submission
or dominion
but will rise up
confounding scheming plans
returning with laughter
bone shaking laughter.
Of course Sarah laughed!

~ Liz Crumlish

Writing stories allows the subversive nature of the supervisory task to emerge and invites a form of naming without judging that frees the story teller to recover insight which becomes possible when imagination is given free rein. And then, embodying the insight gained, a new chapter is waiting to be written.

Fairy tales in Supervision

In 'The Seven Basic Plots: Why We Tell Stories', Christopher Booker explores storytelling through the eyes of the Swiss psychiatrist and psychoanalyst, Carl Jung. In Jung's analysis, regardless of the number of characters in a story, it is typically the hero that is given most attention. Other actors play their parts but it is the hero's call to adventure, his or her initial successes, frustrations and ultimately their overcoming of adversity that are prioritised.

Against the backdrop of fairy tales and epic stories, supervision offers supervisees an opportunity to explore their own 'heroic' journeys from first fervour through their frustrations to their conquering of adversity. When working with stories in supervision Graham Greene's wisdom is worth remembering:

> 'A story has no beginning or end: arbitrarily one chooses that moment of experience from which to look back or from which to look ahead.'

Focusing in on those aspects of the story which have most resonance for supervisees (rather than asking them to recount the plot from beginning to end in a linear fashion) helps supervisees connect more deeply with the story.

> 'It's like Goldilocks and the Three Bears all over again' ... ever since I started in this new job, there seems to always be someone who puts nothing in - doesn't shop for the porridge, doesn't make the porridge, doesn't wash the bowls after the porridge but simply eats the porridge. That's what it's like at work just now.'

The stories supervisees bring do not always have happy endings. Seldom do the protagonists live happily ever after. Some supervisory stories are ongoing and interminable. Others expand with new twists and turns. Some stories leave supervisors eager for the next chapter. Others bear all the hallmarks of tragic loss and grief. But even when story lines seem given and fixed, Viktor Frankl reminds us that 'between stimulus and response there is a space. In that space is our power to choose our response'.[97] Without collapsing supervision into personal therapy, supervisors have a role to play in helping supervisees unearth and own their own stories. And then, when stories are owned, helping them write themselves into the plot rather than watch it unfold before them. At times supervision even allows supervisees to write their own 'brave new endings'.[98]

---

[97] Viktor E. Frankl, (1959,2006) *Man's Search for Meaning* , Beacon Press 65–67, 112.
[98] Brené Brown, (2015) *Rising Strong,* London: Penguin Random House.

To follow up

Bolton, G. (2007) Victoria Field and Kate Thompson (eds) (2007) *Writing Works: A Resource Handbook for Therapeutic Writing Workshops and Activities*, London: Jessica Kingsley

Bolton, G., Field, V. and Thompson, K. (eds) (2011) *Writing Routes: A Resource Handbook of Therapeutic Writing*, London: Jessica Kingsley

McCormack, D. (2010) The Transformative power of Journalling: Reflective Practice as Self-Supervision in Benefiel and Holton, *The Soul of Supervision*, New York: Morehouse.

Thompson, K. (2010) *Using your Journal as a Supervision Tool*, Wheatbridge Colorado: Therapeutic Writing Institute

Walton, H. (2015) *Not Eden: Spiritual Life Writing for This World*, London: SCM

Living link to learning

A supervisor is the living link to learning

the storyteller who,
for each chapter read,
listens to two chapters
read back

the opener of spaces
for understanding and
ah ha's

the navigator with no hand on the wheel
(but) guiding discovery

the wise reflector
in the here and now
as they hear
the there and then

The trusted supervisor learns from supervisees
and submits to a higher value
beyond integrity
knowing

that life will talk sweet words of wisdom
to whomever will turn their ear

~ Andy Gillies

Multi-modal Exploration

Each art must nourish the other, each one can add to the other. And I would take into writing what I learned from dancing, what I learned from music, what I learned from design.

Anais Nin[99]

For ease of explanation, this book has introduced creative modalities under the headings of Art & Imagery; Sound and Music; Movement & Embodiment; Drama & Role and Language & Story. In the practice of supervision those boundaries need not be observed. In fact, boundary crossing is sometimes required. As we have seen earlier a visual depiction of the supervisory issue being brought to the session may well be explored further through a written or spoken dialogue or indeed danced out. A sound made in the eliciting and focusing phase of the session could be amplified by the creation of a visual installation made up of cloths and objects. So too an authentic movement expressing the supervisee's relationship to work could be teased out in role reversal either by the supervisor or by members of a group.

Two examples of multi-modal exploration follow. The first is drawn from individual supervision. The second from group supervision.

---

[99] Anais Nin *A Woman Speaks* quoted in Rogers, (1993) *Creative Connection*, 43

Multi-modal Individual Supervision

Fatima came to supervision via Zoom unsure what to focus on. Not knowing how to 'fill the hour' had left her anxious. Having acknowledged her anxiety I invited her to take a moment to simply notice her breathing and allow it to support her.

I invited her to turn her camera off if she wanted to and to spend some time practicing double breathing.

To indicate that she was ready to begin I invited her to sound her singing bowl and switch her camera back on.

Once she switched her camera on, I invited her to scan the room she was in and allow her eyes to land on something that could support her for the session.

A framed art print on her wall caught her attention.

I invited her to approach the image to see it more closely.

'What is happening?' I asked.

'My eye is drawn to the edges where the light evaporates' she answered.

'And what happens when the light evaporates?' I asked.

'The rest is trust' she said.

'And where does that take you?' I asked

'To a staff meeting yesterday.' She answered.

(I keep silence.)

'Actually the light is not evaporating. Under the new management it feels like it is, but it's not because I won't let it'.

And where are you now? I ask.

'My eye has moved to the frame.'

'What is it about the frame?'

'Its solid, it offers good boundaries, its dusty, it needs a good clean'

'Anything else about the frame?'

'Yes, without it the picture wouldn't stay on the wall.'

'Where does this take you as you consider your work right now?' …

'Whenever you are ready please come back to your chair'

Multi-modal Group Supervision

In *The Four Elements*, Lia Zografou offers a quick-fire method of representation based on the philosophy and technique of playback theatre which she developed out of working with very large supervision groups. The aim is to offer supervisees short, immediate, thought-provoking responses to stimulate further reflection.

The Four Elements Group Supervision

The exploratory area is set up with 6 chairs. These are occupied by:

The *Teller* (supervisee) who is grappling with an issue.

The *Visual Artist* who is the member of the group who will offer a visual response to the Teller's narration. This can be abstract or figurative, a simple squiggle to a more elaborate image.

The *Mover* who is the member of the group who will use movement, with the help of cloths, to offer an image in space.

The *Poet/Singer/Storyteller* who is the person who will offer a few lines of a poem or a song or a popular story or fairytale.

The *Colleague* who will offer reflections, examples or anecdotes from similar experiences in their working life.

The *Supervisor* who holds the ritual structure of the exploration by calling 'let's watch' to mark the beginning of a response, ensures that the representations are short and succinct and elicits the Teller's impression(s) in the end. This role is occupied by the actual supervisor of the group.

Once the Teller has shared his/her concern, the four group members will in turn offer their responses which should be no more than 1 minute in length. At the end of the representation the Teller absorbs their offers and shares how his/her reflection has shifted as a result. The rest of the group observe but are not involved in discussion.

During a group session the chairs are occupied by various members of the group so that, ideally, everyone has had the opportunity to share in everyone's explorations in some capacity. After everyone has had a go, a group discussion/feedback takes place whereby supervisory foci are identified, questions clarified and the work continues in more depth. [100]

---

[100] See chapter 4 on this approach in Chesner & Zografou (2013), *Creative Supervision Across Modalities,* London: Jessica Kingsley, 59-70.

Who are the Supervisors?

Armed with the tools
of my newly learned skills
I rocked up ready
to dispense wisdom
Surrounded by shiny new toys
and all the paraphernalia
that would ensure
I made room to put the creative
into creative supervision
I looked for approval
and compliance
from those who would experience
my learning
And, in the first hour
I was blown away
by the insight of my supervisee
who taught me about grace in adversity
and who showed me the importance
of fostering resilience
that embodies hope
for transformation.

Next time, I thought,
next time, I'll get it right
I'll listen well
and find a way
to be brilliant
and to be sure, my supervisee
needed me to hear
not so that I would understand
but so that she might be held
while she got to the core

of her own process
and I learned the sacred art
of holding space for another

And so it went on
as encounter followed encounter
I moved from being host
and fount of wisdom
to being guest
and student of teachers
who vulnerably shared their gifts with me
inviting me on a mutual journey
of insight and discovery
as,
together,
we shared our brokenness
and bore witness
to the possibility of healing and growth
taking risks together
recapturing vision that had become peripheral
to inform the present
and co-create a walkway into the future.

~ Liz Crumlish

Ignoring the Sat Nav

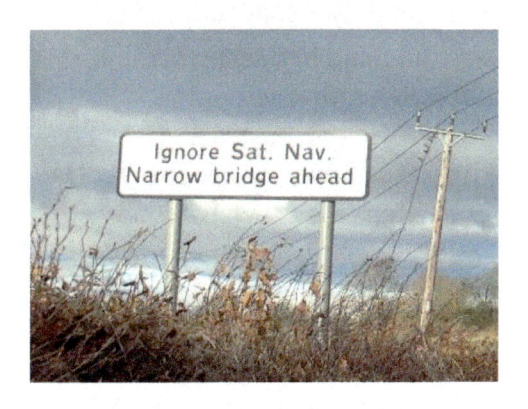

Sometimes it is necessary
to ignore the sat nav
to let go
of our frameworks
and theories
and even our shiny new tools
so that we may simply
hold an hospitable space
that invites adventure

Sometimes it is right
to tune out
the voices in our heads
the pictures in our minds
of how the journey goes
so that we can venture
into exploration
without a map

For the contemplative art
of listening to ignite
and the soulful guddling in role and context

rarely conform to narrow confines
but spill over
touching and transforming
all in their path

And we can only ignore the Sat Nav
when we know just what
we are letting go of
and
taking courage in both hands
consent to journey
off the beaten track
to reach a destination unknown
yet longed for.

~ Liz Crumlish

Online Supervision: Factors to Consider

Supervising online was resisted by many practitioners until it became a necessity due to the restrictions about meeting in person imposed by the Coronavirus pandemic. 'It won't be the same', 'the quality of presence will be weakened', 'we won't have all the cues that we get from body language, shifts in movement or changes in eye contact.'

Forced to adapt many supervisors now report - while still not their preferred mode of relating – a quality of relating that goes to greater depth than in person meeting. Some of this can be put down to the fact that supervisees are often logging on to supervision from their own homely environments in which levels of safety and familiarity positively contribute to the hospitality and containment of the session. Others would point to the loss of the privacy afforded by the supervisor's consulting room which is hard to replicate when supervisees do not live alone. Others again report the lack of transitional space and time between home life, work life and the supervisory space. 'I miss the journey here' said one supervisee 'it's where I prepare for our sessions. Now I find myself going from one thing to another without sufficient thought.' The notes which follow are offered to help supervisors be aware of the pitfalls which working online can offer and which require attention if we are to foster a space (on line) that is conducive for reflection and transformative learning.

Pre-session preparation

Beware of the temptation to spend less time getting ready because you are already at your desk (reading emails etc) Uninterrupted space is as important online as it would be if you were meeting face to face but might need negotiation with others in your home or workspace (phone ringing, fax machine, callers at door etc.)

Since online supervision (especially for those who are not familiar with technology) may raise additional anxieties, ensure that you take the time to notice any pre-transferences you may have concerning the person you are about to 'meet' or about the session itself so that you begin not in anxiety but from a settled place which can truly make room for the other

To compensate for the lack of immediate presence online platforms do not afford, you might like to spend an empathic moment placing yourself in the shoes of your supervisee imagining their professional world, or their feelings about coming to see you online etc.

Technology

Before agreeing to offer supervision online make sure you have a stable and fast internet connection. If your Wi-Fi is unstable using an ethernet cable may help.

Programmes running in the background are likely to slow things down on your device.

When connections are poor, or video freezes, switching the video off often helps.

Make sure you have agreed in advance a back-up plan if the connection fails (for example to continue by telephone).

Make sure email pings (and similar) sound alerts are switched off to avoid distractions on both sides.

Ensure the session is not being broadcast to others or inadvertently recorded.

Decide whether you will use earphones or a headset or not.

Environment

Since many people associate online platforms with social media, be especially aware not to lessen your professional standards by for example connecting from your bedroom or from a part of your house or office to which others may need access.

Consider what is in your line of vision (remembering that supervisees only see whatever is behind you). Similarly pay attention to what is in your line of sight. Will seeing it support your availability for the supervisee or distract your attention away from them?

What do you want to show or not show in your environment? (ie pay attention to what lies behind you that will be broadcast online). Think carefully also about what in your space is yours and what is not yours to show. Similarly be clear with supervisees about what they are showing of their environment.

Think carefully about how you will attend to the supervisory role of hospitality in an online virtual space?

Are you ready for creativity should it seem appropriate ie do you have things to hand you could use? Are you ready to encourage your supervisee to use creative methods *even if* you cannot see what they are doing. You could for example keep on your desk top a set of image cards which you can use by sharing screen. You might like to send supervisee a set and ask them to also keep them accessible for use in sessions.

Impact on the Supervisory Relationship

You may need to prepare your supervisee for online supervision (practicalities, audibility, visibility, agreements about who calls who etc.)

Since supervisees are entitled to be late or to not show up it is best to have supervisees contact you (this parallels knocking your door etc) rather than you sitting in their online waiting room.

Sessions often begin with variations on 'Can you see me? Can you hear me?' Many of these openings contain some expression of anxiety that the parties involved might not connect or that our connection may not be reliable or our connection may fail. It is important to hear such expressions both literally and as a possible commentary on the supervisory relationship. Be attentive therefore to issues of the working alliance, transferences from the past etc.

Do not begin until you have checked that you can both see/hear each sufficiently well. (If you begin a session seeing only a person's face from the nose upwards it could be interruptive to ask them later to adjust their camera angle). Similarly, make sure the device both parties are using is placed in a steady position rather than being hand held and wobbly.

Once you have dealt with the technology and established a connection it is often worth making an *explicit* starting point e.g. 'Now that we can see and hear each other let's just take a moment to enter this space. Let me know when you are ready to begin.'

Do not as supervisor take control or responsibility for issues pertaining to digital technology. You are responsible for facilitating reflection. You are not responsible for the quality or speed of your supervisee's broadband. Be aware of taking responsibility for things that are not yours.

Clicks, interference, delays in sound, freezing of images while not inevitable are likely to arise so you might want to establish a way of signalling you can't hear or see or missed something before you even begin.

Similarly when the Wi-Fi signal is interrupted you might want to make more use of playing back what you heard before you were disconnected or the screen froze than you might do face to face.

Where there is a time delay, either party may inadvertently talk over the other or not quite catch something. Do not hesitate to check what you missed or verify what you heard if it serves the supervisee to do so.

Do not allow technology to lessen your ability to be present, or to constrict the range of methods you might to explore something. You *can* do role work, 2 chair work, small world, movement and music online.

Silence has its place in supervision. Do not rule it out just because you are online.

Announce absences from the screen. For example if at the end of the session you need to look up your electronic diary to arrange the next meeting tell the person you are switching screens otherwise they may simply see you looking away from them and typing.

Transition

Described as the space between trapezes
Not possible without a letting go
Difficult enough when it is chosen
Even harder when imposed
And when I find myself suspended
in that space between
who will encourage me onward
to continue on the arc
that takes me further than I have ever gone?
And, if that time
of being suspended in mid-air
is longer than anticipated
who will risk
stepping into the void alongside me?
Who will join me
in that wild and precarious space
that speaks of possibility
that invites creativity
that is pregnant with potential
Who will hear my story
help me re-member
and commit
to the next part of the journey
as I reach for a touching point
that remembers what was
celebrates what is
and transforms what will be?

~ Liz Crumlish

Appreciation

These, these are the ones who have walked with me
where no one else would go.

These are the ones
who have not refused to look upon me.

These are the ones who have come near
when others would not.

These are the ones who have shared my story
of pain and joy and hopes and dreams unfulfilled
and helped me rise again to the challenge
of your call to serve.

These are the ones who have shown me your face.
And these are the ones who have seen your face
reflected in me.

These are the ones who have touched me,
revealing your Divine tenderness.
These are the ones who have incarnated
compassionate love.
These are the ones who have mediated your presence.

These are your gift to me and I tremble with joy.
For all these people and their place in my life,
I give thanks.

~ Source Unknown

Continue

My wish for you is that you continue

Continue
To attend to your own soul, role and context
so that others might engage
reflexively with theirs

Continue
To do your own hard work
so that you have capacity to hold space for others
as they do theirs

Continue
To show up with all of you
joining God
in the sacred art of listening to ignite

Continue
To use your creativity
to unearth creativity in another
and to release wisdom
that's just momentarily out of sight

Continue
To learn from those
who trust you
with their stories
and with their brokenness
so that, together, you may experience growth.

Continue
To risk wondering
pitching your offerings
of insight tentatively
allowing the other
to engage or reframe

Continue
To walk alongside others
keeping out of the way
as they find the power
of their own agency
and discern the next steps

Continue
To advocate for this restorative work
for the health and well-being
of those who serve
and for those who are served

Continue
To attend to covenant
and boundaries
in order to create brave spaces
in which vision might be enlarged

Continue
And by doing so
you and those with whom you work
will know the power
of transformative space.

adapted from a poem of Maya Angelou
by Liz Crumlish

Reading about Pastoral Supervision

Broughton, G. (2021) *A Practical Christology for Pastoral Supervision*, London: Routledge

Dixon Cameron, H. (2018) *Living in the Gaze of God: Supervision and Ministerial Flourishing*, Norwich: SCM

Jones, L. C. (2019) *The Care of Souls: Reflections on the Art of Pastoral Supervision*, Eugene, OR: Wipf & Stock.

Leach, J. (2020) *A Charge to Keep: Reflective Supervision and the Renewal of Christian Leadership*, Higher Education & Ministry Publishing

Leach, J. & Paterson, M. (2015) *Pastoral Supervision: A Handbook*, 2nd edition, London: SCM.

de Long, W. (2009) *Courageous Conversations: The teaching and learning of pastoral supervision*, University Press of America.

Paterson, M. and Rose, J. (2014) *Enriching Ministry: Pastoral Supervision in Practice*, London: SCM

Paterson, M. (2020) *Between a Rock and a Hard Place: Pastoral Supervision Revisited and Revisioned*, Edinburgh: IPSRP.

Pohly, K. (2001) *Transforming the Rough Places: The Ministry of Supervision*, 2nd Edition, Franklin TN: Providence House.

Reflective Practice: Formation and Supervision in Ministry. An open access journal journals.sfu.ca/rpfs/index.php/rpfs

Reviving the Spirit: The Gift of Pastoral Supervision, Special edition of St Mark's Review No. 254, December 2020 (4). St Mark's Canberra.

Ward, F. (2005) *Lifelong Learning: Theological Education and Supervision*, London: SCM.

Reading about Creativity in Supervision

Bownas, J. and Fredman, G. (2017) *Working with Embodiment in Supervision: A Systemic Approach*, London: Routledge.

Carpendale, M. (2011) *A Traveller's Guide to Art Therapy Supervision*, Victoria, Canada: Trafford Publishing

Chesner, A. and Zografou (2013) *Creative Supervision Across Modalities*, London: Jessica Kingsley

Fish, B. (2016) *Art-Based Supervision: Cultivating Therapeutic Insight Through Imagery*, London: Routledge

Jones, P. and Dokter, D. (2008) *Supervision of Dramatherapy*, London: Routledge

Lahad, M. (2000) *Creative Supervision: The Use of Expressive Arts in Supervision and Self Supervision*, London: Jessica Kingsley

Odell-Miller, H. and Richards, E. (2007) *Supervision of Music Therapy: A Theoretical and Practical Handbook*, London: Routledge

Payne, H. (2008) *Supervision of Dance Movement Psychotherapy: A Practitioner's Handbook*, London: Routledge

Rogers, N. (1993) *The Creative Connection: Expressive Arts as Healing*, London: PCCS

Schuck, C. and Wood, J. (2011) *Inspiring Creative Supervision*, London: Jessica Kingsley

Silverstone, L. (2009) *Art Therapy Exercises: Inspirational & Practical Ideas to Stimulate the Imagination*, London: Jessica Kingsley

Weld, N. (2012) *A practical guide to transformative supervision for the helping professions: Amplifying insight*, London: Jessica Kingsley

Williams, A. (1995) *Visual and Active Supervision: Roles, Focus, Technique*, London: Norton

Reading about Supervision in general

Beddoe, L. and Davys, A. (2016) *Challenges in Professional Supervision: Current Themes and Models for Practice*, London: Jessica Kingsley

Benefiel, M. and Holton, G. (2010) *The Soul of Supervision: Integrating Practice and Theory*, New York: Morehouse,

Carroll, M. (2014) *Effective Supervision for the Helping Professions*, London: Sage

Creaner. M. (2014) *Getting the Best out of Supervision in Counselling & Psychotherapy: A Guide for the Supervisee*, London: Sage.

Davys, A. and Beddoe, L. (2010) *Best Practice in Supervision: A Guide for the Helping Professions*, London: Jesssica Kingsley.

Hawkins, P. & McMahon, A. (2020) *Supervision in the Helping Professions* 5th edition, Buckingham: Open University Press, 2006

Hewson, D. and Carroll, M. (2016) *Reflective Practice in Supervision*, Hazlebrook, NSW: MoshPit.

Moore, B. (2016) *Reflexive Supervision: A workbook for Learning within and across Professions*, KDP.

Page, S. and Wosket, V. (2001) Supervising the Counsellor: A Cyclical Model, 2nd Edition. Hove: Routledge.

Ryan, S. (2004) *Vital Practice: Stories from the healing arts: The homeopathic and supervisory way*, Porland: Sea Change

Shohet, R. (2008) ed., *Passionate Supervision*, London: Jessica Kingsley

Shohet, R. and Shohet, J. (2020) *In love with supervision: Creating transformative conversations*, Monmouth: PCCS.

Supervision Journal

Droichead, Journal of the Supervisors Association of Ireland https://saivision.ie/

Author Index

Angelou, Maya 196, 220
Anzaldúa Gloria 89
Arrien, Angue 137

Bazely, Mogs 6, 60
Bloomfield, Frances 32
Bonhoeffer, Dietrich 144
Booker, Christopher 198
British Medical Association 24
Broughton, Geoff 19
Brown Taylor, Barbara 26
Brown, Brene 34
Byock, Ira 60

Campbell, Don 138
Carroll, Michael 57
Chapman Campbell, Alexander 139
Chessner, Anna 84
Covey, Steve 88
Crumlish, Liz 7, 8, 26, 53, 93, 111, 129, 146, 161, 177, 196, 208, 210, 217, 220, 237

Davis, Noel 116
Dickinson, Emily vi
Doerrfeld, Cori 194

Francis, Pope 24
Frankl, Viktor E. 189, 199
Fredman, Glenda 158, 181, 222
Frost, Robert 21
Frost, Seena 121, 132
Furth, Gregg M. 124

Gendlin, E. T. 148, 158
Gillies, Andy 201
Gorton, Catriona 56
Greene, Graham 198
Grosz, Stephen 136
Grove, David 179

Hall, Diana 41
Hawkins, Peter 24, 46, 52, 62, 223
Holloway, Elizabeth 101

Jeffers, Oliver 194
Joseph, Julie 154

Kandinsky, Vassily 136
Kearins, Helen 48
Kline, Nancy 68, 172, 190

Lahad, Mooli 44
Leach, Jane 106
Levitt, Olga 149
Litchfield, David 195
Lunan, Maggie 29
Landy, Robert 162

Mackesy, Charlie 195
Maitland, Sara vii
McDonough, Andrew 194
Mettler, Barbara 147
Moore, Bobby 1
Moreno, Jacob L. 162
Mosteghanemi, Ahlam 193
Murray, Sarah 134

Nin, Anais 202
Nine beats Collective 39

O'Donohue, John 59

Pandian, Ali 73
Parker Palmer, J. 20
Pärt, Arvo 139
Paterson, Michael 64, 69
Patton, John 16
Polwarth, Karine v
Richter, Max 143

Rogers, Natalie 102, 120
Rumi, Jalāl ad-Dīn Mohammad 34
Ryan, Sheila 100

Shohet, Robin 24, 46, 50, 52, 62
Silverstein, Shiel 194
Spangler, David 33
Speechley, Margaret 35
Starr, Mirabai 7
Spolin, Viola 169
Stuart, David 184

Tempest Williams, Terry 79, 187, 188

Weil, Simone 136
Wells, Sam 37
Williams, Antony vi, 97, 163, 197
Wintour, Joyce 45

Zografou, Lia 103, 205, 239

Subject Index

Art   120ff

beginnings (in supervision)   51, 79-80, 151
body scan   150
body shake   148
body sculpt   174
breathing exercises   78, 148-50
bridging and enacting   76, 87, 89, 127, 173-74, 191

cantus firmus 144
chair work   168
clean language 179
communication by impact   156
context   16, 18, 20, 24-5, 143
contracting   36-8, 57, 152
covenant   38-9, 51, 57
creative modalities   42, 77, 86, 96-8, 102-09, 112, 129

discernment   110
drama   162
drama, internalised   106, 167
drawing   106, 123-27, 132

eliciting and focusing   75, 81-2, 140, 153, 181
embodied modalities 98
embodiment   147ff
endings   60-62, 199
experimentation   170
exploring and imagining 76, 83, 156

fairy tales   172, 198, 203

felt sense 158
first meeting 36, 43
focusing 75, 81-2, 140, 158, 181
four elements 205

guided drawing 126

hospitality 49, 51, 66, 75, 77-8, 83, 85, 90
hosting and containing 75

ignite, listen to 71-2, 190, 209, 219
imagery & art 120-21, 126
image cards 10, 21, 44, 82, 214
ink polaroids 184
Inner Wise Guide 173-4
internal dialogue 112, 172
internalised drama 106, 167
interrupt, listen to 70, 72

jaw, softening 148

language 71, 81, 101, 106-07, 179-80, 187-192
listening to ignite 71-72, 189
listening to interrupt 70, 72
listening to understand 70, 72

modalities 27, 42, 77, 84, 86, 96-8, 102, 104, 106, 109, 112, 129, 202
movement 87, 147, 153, 202
multimodal exploration 202
music 136ff, 145

noticing 65-66, 68, 86, 124
objections (to creative supervision) 102-104

outdoors 128, 152
parts of self 108
pastoral 18, 19, 25, 27
polaroids, ink 183
power 17, 19, 37, 39, 53, 55
pre-transference 33-4
projective modalities 96-7, 105-06, 120, 167, 196

realising 44, 64-66, 68
relationship 36ff, 60
restorative 92, 162
reviewing 51-2, 76
reviewing and closing 76, 90-1, 166, 192
role 20, 98, 143, 162
role of supervisor 19, 140, 172
role modalities 98
role reversal 84, 129, 164-6

sat nav for supervision 75, 85, 209
sculpting, body 174
seven eyes 46-48
showing up 49, 134
six minute journaling 182
small world 44, 52, 72, 89, 114-15, 216
somatic resonance 156-57
soul 20, 87
Soul Collage® 131-12
sound 136-45, 201-02
space 14, 26, 40, 174, 176, 189, 196
story, stories 177ff, 182, 188, 193-9
supervision, definition 16
supervisory process 73ff, 85
supervisory relationship 36, 63, 68, 214
supervisory space 182, 196, 211

textiles 129
three kinds of listening 69-72
three levels of seeing 63-66, 122, 140, 165
tracking and monitoring 71, 76, 85-7, 163
tracking language 180
transition 91, 139, 175, 182, 211, 217

unconscious 46, 58, 157
understand, listen to 70-72

visual images 120, 123
vocalisation 138
vulnerability 53, 55

weaving 35, 101, 130-32, 196
wellbeing 19, 27, 33, 68, 88
wonder 64, 68, 74, 84, 86, 121-2, 124-25, 134
wordles 191
writing in pencil 188
writing a different ending 189
writing in supervision 184-87

Index of poems

A recognition of what I bring   45
A space filled with grace   26
Against the tide   28
All tuned up and ready to go   146

Before meeting for the first time   35

Continue   219

Discernment   110

I interrupt, I understand, I ignite   69
Ignoring the Sat Nav   209
In the space between us   40
Into this room   134

Living link to learning   201

Newly laid turf   45

On his way elsewhere   177

Power and vulnerability   53
Preparing to host a supervisee   32

Reaching downwards and delving   151
Restorative space   92

Seven Eyes   48
Showing up   134
Supervision as weaving   101
Supervisory space   26

The Supervisor is the living link to learning   201
The supervisory process   73
The then and there   48
The way ahead lies trapped   8
These, these are the ones   218
Three kinds of listening   69
Three levels of seeing   64
Thrust into this space   53
Transition   217
Trusting my competence   55
Two vessels   29
Two women walked   160

Unicycling juggler   55

When all of me shows up for you   50
When I can 'get over myself'   7
Who are the supervisors?   207
Why did Sarah laugh?   196
Write in pencil   188

Contributors

Suzanne Aitken is an HCPC registered Dramatherapist, and NMC registered Mental Health Nurse Specialist currently working in a busy Child and Adolescent Mental Health Service Trauma team. She has a thriving Supervision Practice, offering Clinical Supervision to Arts Therapists, Psychotherapists and Play Therapists and Supervision and Reflective Practice to staff teams across Residential Care settings for looked after children and young people. She has been part of a small team developing a Masters training in Dramatherapy, the first of its kind in Scotland.

Mogs Bazely is a counsellor, psychotherapist and lecturer. She currently spends most of her time supervising and training those who work in faith – based contexts to become pastoral supervisors. Having shared a clergy household with her husband for 35 years, she is keen to see people of faith trained and supported to thrive in their vocations. She sees pastoral supervision as an essential discipline, modelled for us by Jesus in company with his disciples; a collaborative learning exercise, a regular rest stop, to acknowledge and explore the joys and challenges of ministry in the presence of the Spirit.

Frances Bloomfield is a minister and also both a counsellor and pastoral supervisor working in her own private practice. She loves the creativity of supervision and the way in which it can unexpectedly open up understanding of both the present and a positive way forward.

Andy Gillies is a healthcare chaplain and national trainer for Values Based Reflective Practice working in Scotland. As a supervisor he works mainly with clinicians around the disconnect between the why and how of caring for patients. He is passionate about creating spaces where the golden thread of soul and role can connect with one another.

Catriona Gorton has been in Baptist ministry for around twenty years, having previously been a consultant engineer. She serves an inclusive, multi-cultural congregation in Glasgow and mentors newly accredited ministers. Beyond church, she is a peer support volunteer for a cancer charity. She also enjoys walking, reading, drinking tea, and cuddling her pet cats!

Lynne Grahame is an art therapist who has worked with young people and their families in the voluntary sector over the last 20 years. Currently working in private practise with adults and young people. Lynne provides creative supervision and reflective practice to student therapists, and therapists working with children, young people and their families in mental health, education and fostering services.

Diana Hall is a priest serving a Scottish Episcopal and Methodist church, and working with people discerning a vocation to ordained ministry. Her supervision practice is cross-professional, offering hospitable spaces in which to reflect on the joys, challenges and complexities of work. She believes good supervision can open the door to an experience of 'life in all its fullness' in the professional context, to the benefit of those we serve.

Julie Joseph OBE is a movement psychotherapist and the founder of a therapeutic child care company which offers care and education for young people in the UK. Her company specialises in working with some of the most challenging young people in the country, many of whom have significant histories of trauma and abuse. Julie has over 20 years' experience of working with both the young people and the staff who care for them. Her supervision approach is a blend of the creative modalities with a strong focus of embodiment and somatic resonance. She works as a supervisor within her own company as well as having a private practice offering both individual and group supervision.

Helen Kearins is a Sister of Mercy with a background in school, adult and Social Justice Education. She has recently moved into assisting with the training of Volunteer Pastoral Carers in the hospitals in the far South Coast of NSW (Australia). Her supervision work is with these Pastoral Carers, some individual clients and groups of semi-retired Sisters of Mercy in Pastoral Reflective Circles. She sees supervision as creating a space where the other can reflect on their work in the world

Fiona Kernohan works freelance in Psychotherapy, Counselling and Clinical supervision. Her work is primarily in the field of generic mental health with adults, young people and children in both community and educational settings. She also provides mental health and wellbeing training. Fiona lives in East Lothian and works throughout Scotland.

Markus Lange is a Rabbi, practicing Drama Therapist and adult educator. He has a special interest in working with primary school children as well as in providing multi-professional approaches to therapeutic group work in hospice/palliative care and mental health services. He is also a Playback Theatre practitioner and enjoys learning more about himself (and others) in comedy improvization, social clowning and puppetry workshops.

Maggie Lunan trained as a teacher and was manager of Christian Aid Scotland's Education and Youth team. Receiving spiritual direction led her to train in accompaniment and to offer a pilot accompaniment project within the Church of Scotland for newly ordained ministers. Her supervision practice has come at a time of transition in the Church. She values the opportunity to work with ministers as they express their fears and their hopes in this time of change.

Kristin MacDonald is a classically-trained soprano and a music therapist. She works with children and adults in educational and health care setting and in a High Secure psychiatric hospital. Kristin offers individual supervision on a free-lance basis with music therapists with a particular focus on creative methods of supervision.

Sarah Murray is the Provost (priest) of Inverness Cathedral with the pastoral care and oversight of the congregation and in to the wider community. As a supervisor she hopes to work cross-professionally, with an interest in group supervision as well as 1-1. Sarah sees supervision as a place to explore work enabling a wider vision and resetting of the plumb line to provide a good balance between life and work, ensuring that each person can be their best in both place.

Ali Pandian is a Senior Healthcare Chaplain working for NHS Lanarkshire. She uses pastoral supervision with NHS colleagues and Church of Scotland employees to help them explore the connections between their values/calling and the work they currently do. She is enabled to connect with others in this way partly because she has experienced first-hand the power of having space intentionally set aside and held by a trusted and skilled supervisor in her own regular supervision sessions. She regards these sessions as necessary and precious.

Margaret Speechley offers pastoral supervision, support, and counselling mainly for those in church leadership. She believes that honest and trusted relationships are the vital keys to good leadership. For Margaret, supervision offers an invaluable and confidential time and space for leaders to make sense of the issues they face. Margaret is based in Adelaide, Australia.

Stephanie Turner is a Dramatherapist working in NHS forensic services in Scotland. She is a Programme Leader on the newly validated MSc Dramatherapy at Queen Margaret University and works privately as a Dramatherapist and registered supervisor across diverse sectors.

Aisling Vorster is a music therapist specialising in work with children and families in schools, health services, residential and charitable organisations. Aisling provides cross-professional supervision and reflective practice sessions, combining creative and verbal resources, across a range of disciplines including teaching, general practice, mental health services and allied health professions.

Joyce Wintour is a counsellor and counselling supervisor with experience of working privately and in Healthcare contexts. Recently she has become interested in Cross Professional Supervision, partly with a view to transferring existing skills to an educational setting, by offering support to people working in schools. Joyce values the privileges and rich learning engendered by the supervisory relationship, endeavouring always to expand the safe space she offers supervisees and to find creative ways of together deepening their explorations and reflections.

Lia Zografou is a Therapist, Supervisor, Coach and playback practitioner working in the fields of therapy, education, professional training & business consulting. She is committed to supporting clients achieve optimal performance with emotional balance, mindful choice and masterly communication. She is co-editor of Chesner and Zografou (2013) *Creative Supervision Across Modalities*, London: Jessica Kingsley.

About the authors

Michael Paterson is the Founding Director of the Institute of Pastoral Supervision and Reflective Practice. He first trained as a counselling supervisor and then, ten years later, as a Cross-Professional creative supervisor at the London Centre for Psychodrama. He is the co-architect (with Ewan Kelly) of Values Based Reflective Practice (VBRP) which supports frontline NHS staff in Scotland. Michael's publications include: *Enriching Ministry: Pastoral Supervision in Context* (2014) with Jessica Rose; *Pastoral Supervision: A Handbook* (2nd edition, 2015) with Jane Leach and *Between a Rock and a Hard Place: Pastoral Supervision Revisited and Revisioned* (2020). Michael is the programme lead for the IPSRP Diploma in Cross-Professional Supervision in Scotland.

Liz Crumlish has served in Health Care Chaplaincy and in Parish Ministry. For the last few years she has worked in renewal and pioneering, mentoring leaders and congregations through cultural change. She is a Board Member of RevGalBlogPals, a global network that seeks to support and amplify the voices of women in ministry. Liz is a regular blogger offering biblical and theological reflections in poetic form www.liz-vicarofdibley.blogspot.com
She has contributed to various publications, including *There's a Woman in the Pulpit* Ed Martha Spong (2015) and *Seeing Afresh: Learning from Fresh Expressions of Church* Ed David McCarthy (2019). As an associate of IPSRP, she co-teaches the Diploma in Cross Professional Supervision.

The Institute of Pastoral Supervision & Reflective Practice

The Institute of Pastoral Supervision & Reflective Practice is an international community of practice committed to training, writing and research in the field of supervision.

With Associates across the world, IPSRP offers professional training courses, continuous professional development workshops and consultancy online and in person.

A full list of Associates and publications can be found at www.ipsrp.org.uk

For details of our Diploma courses and continuing professional development workshops please email training@ipsrp.org.uk

Printed in Great Britain
by Amazon